HOOKED!

America's Passion for Bass Fishing

TEHABI BOOKS

"There was a *fierce* power beneath that *calm* surface."

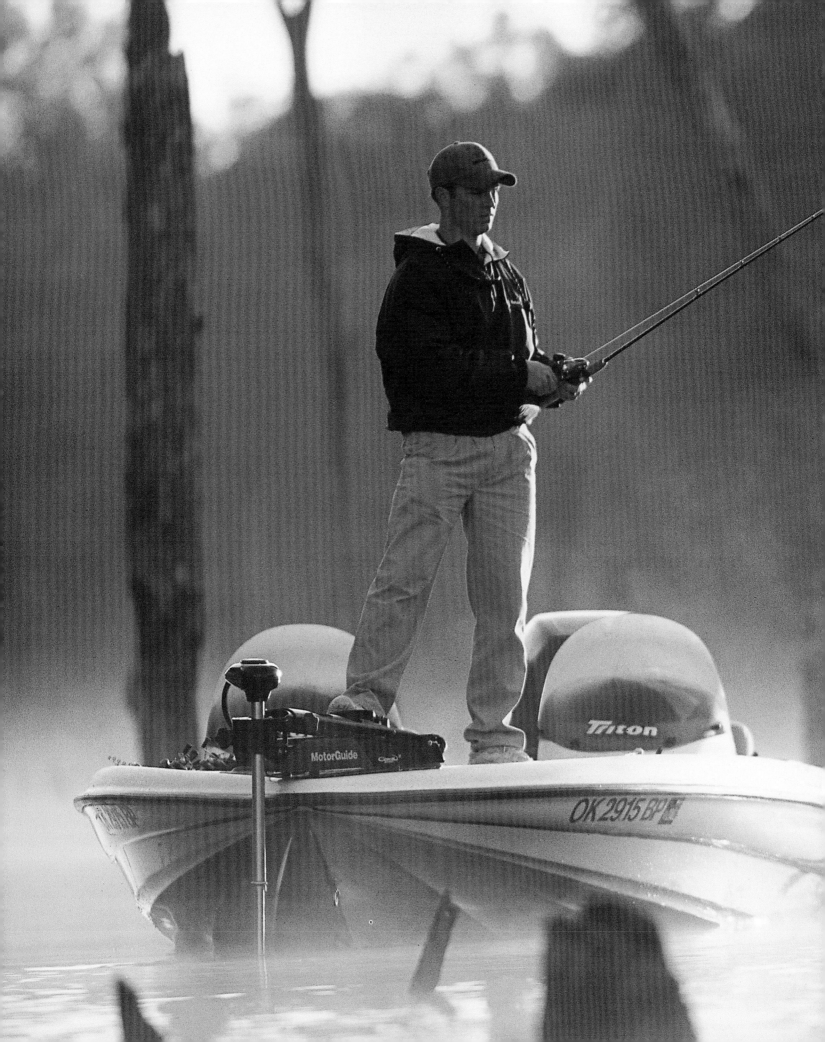

"He **snapped** my line
on a sunken tree last year,
and I **wanted** him."

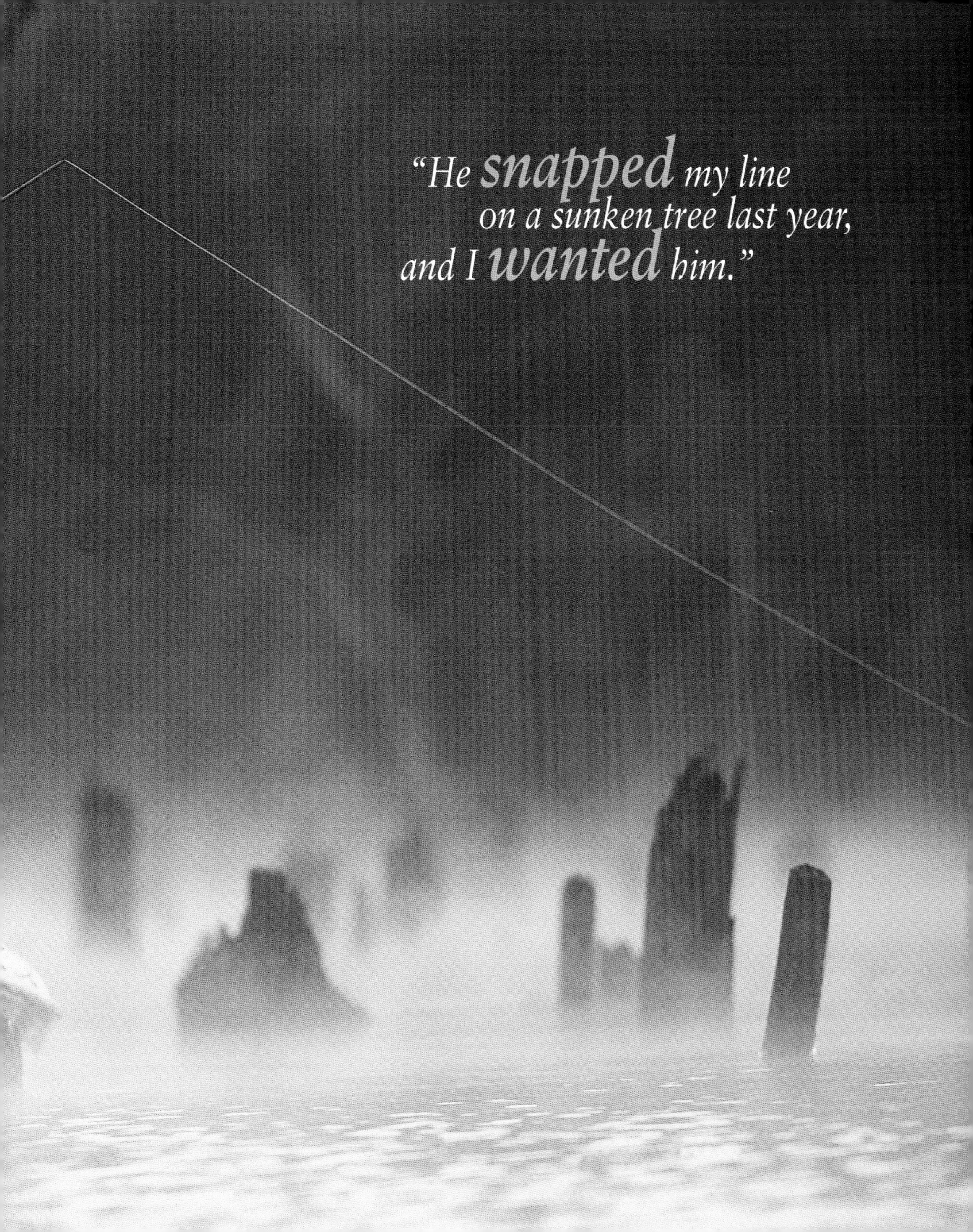

HOO

America's Passion for Bass Fishing

KED!

"It's the **monster,**
the giant,
the *tacklebuster.*"

TEHABI BOOKS

Tehabi Books developed, designed, and produced *Hooked! America's Passion for Bass Fishing,* and has conceived and published many award-winning books that are recognized for their strong literary and visual content. Tehabi works with national and international publishers, corporations, institutions, and nonprofit groups to identify, develop, and implement comprehensive publishing programs. The name *Tehabi* is derived from a Hopi Indian legend and symbolizes the importance of teamwork. Tehabi Books is located in San Diego, California. www.tehabi.com

President **Chris Capen**
Senior Vice President **Tom Lewis**
Vice President, Development **Andy Lewis**
Director, Sales & Marketing **Tim Connolly**
Director, Corporate Publishing & Promotions **Eric Pinkham**
Editorial Director **Nancy Cash**
Art Director **Curt Boyer**
Editor **Terry Spohn**
Consulting Editors **Matt Straw, Doug Hannon, Kevin Mineo, Ed Byrd**
Contributing Authors **Paul Cañada, Rob Crow, Doug Hannon, Kevin Mineo, Matt Straw, Rich Zaleski**
Copyeditor **Robin Witkin**
Proofreader **Marianna Lee**
Indexer **Ken DellaPenta**

Photography credits appear on page 189.

Library of Congress Cataloging-in-Publication Data is available

ISBN 1-887656-80-4
This edition is printed on acid-free paper that meets the American National Standards Institute Z39.48 Standard.

Printed through Dai Nippon Printing Co., Ltd. in Hong Kong.
10 9 8 7 6 5 4 3 2

Table of Contents

Forever Lessons

I once was described as a child in an adult body. I like that. I go to bed a lot of nights hating to stop whatever it is I'm doing. I get up each day looking forward to the adventure. Some nights, I watched the clock for hours, wishing the alarm would start its racket. That's because I chase bass for a living, and I'm grateful for the lifetime of unexpected joy it has given me.

Most folks don't know that my life started out in several directions. I was a second lieutenant in the army, I have a bachelor of science from Maryland State, and, for a year, I taught algebra at a high school in Recife, Brazil. In short, I was given a whole bunch of opportunities to choose a career. That was a really good deal. But even better, I was lucky enough to find out early on that what I really wanted to do with my life was outsmart bass. And I've had fun trying to do that now for more than fifty years.

Bass have been responsible for far greater accomplishments than my small success and gratification. I've witnessed special bondings of families, competitors, and friends that seem to be unique to the pursuit of bass. I've seen countless children given personal direction, character structure, and core values under the guidance of parents and mentors.

And even in the heat of tournament fury, I've watched competitors with hundreds of thousands of dollars at stake help each other against their own best interests. I can't tell you why these things are so wrapped up in the fabric of bass fishing. I can only tell you that it's real and it's good. And the lessons are forever.

Generally, a fisherman's life goes through four stages. In the first stage, the goal is to catch fish—any fish—and lots of 'em. In the second stage, a fisherman works hard to be the best he can be at a particular part of the sport, such as fishing for bass in tournaments. The third stage finds him chasing his favorite fish in trophy sizes. But it's the fourth stage that offers the most payback: when he teaches others to catch a fish and gets the satisfaction of watching them do it. There is no credit to be given for this evolution; it's natural. And if you fish long enough, one stage will follow the other.

Good fortune and bass have always given me more than my share of fun in life. To be able to pass along my knowledge and passion for bass fishing, and to be part of this book and its celebration of the sport I love, is about as perfect as it can get. *Hooked!* presents some of the best writing and information I've seen in its exploration of this sport. It's a genuine, honest perspective to be enjoyed by the expert and nonfisherman alike. In fact, this book gets me so fired up, it makes me want to grab my rod and go meet a bass. Oh, son, I think I'm bit again! ❯ —*Roland Martin*

Predator and Prey

It was close to midnight. I sat, rod in hand, and pondered the silhouette of the dark, calm wetscape, the sweltering heat of a Florida summer, and the silent swarms of hungry mosquitoes that had long since slaked their thirst. From the distance, just beyond the reach of my vision, came a rhythmic lapping sound, almost like a thirsty hound drinking from the edge of the lake. As the sound grew closer, my eyes pried at the darkness until I could barely make out the wake of the black Jitterbug working its way back to the tip of my rod. I lifted the lure up against the sky to check it for floating debris and found instead, hovering on silent wings not three feet in front of me, a huge face with large, pale, dilated eyes. Stifling a cardiac gasp, I flung the lure back into the darkness; after two sloppy laps of the big metal lip came the sound of a wet "click" and then silence.

Seconds later, from directly behind me, a great horned owl rolled out like a retriever. The impact of the two-pound bird traveling thirty miles per hour slamming into the end of my line almost wrenched the rod from my grasp. The recoiling stretch of the 30-pound monofilament ripped the big plug from its talons, shooting it back through the darkness to splash only an arm's length off the port bow. In the frame-by-frame perception of my now-heightened senses, I saw the belly-up Jitterbug slowly roll over and right itself, then disappear into a sudden boil of black water.

Frantically, I spooled a hopeless amount of slack line as a giant bass erupted from the water's surface. Full-bodied and broadside, the airborne form seemed to hang weightless for a moment, washed in the anemic blue light of the rising moon,

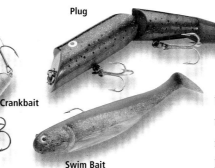

Plug

Crankbait

Swim Bait

before it crashed back into the water, leaving at the surface only my inanimate lure and me. I had a world-class knot in my gut and that indefinable hybrid of hope and desire that I might someday catch such a fish. For now, it would have to be enough just to know that it is out there somewhere and not just a shimmering mirage.

You know the feeling, and you may be drawn to the water for the same reason I am. The fish were biting the day you got married. You're wearing your lucky socks, you're casting that lucky banjo minnow, you didn't pack a banana with your lunch, and you haven't said *p-i-g* since you got into the boat. All that electronic fish-finding gear, those graphite rods, and the big fiberglass sled with its powerful motor can't, by themselves, convince a big one to take your lure. You need that little something extra so you

didn't cut your nails on Friday, you've got your lucky Wacky Worm tied into a slip-knot in your shirt pocket, and you haven't cast across your shadow all morning.

From the boat, you peer down into the watery world that is the bass's undisputed domain. You're straining for a glimpse of it or a hint of one of those hidden places where you know it might be found, concealed among the weeds and outcrops, perfectly blended into its surroundings among the rotting stumps, as still as a rock, waiting and watching for prey. But you're not looking for just any bass. It's the monster, the giant, the tacklebuster, the solitary, the elusive, the unattainable one. It's the unrealizable dream that you carry out and return home with every day you spend on the water.

That dream is crystallized in the one word in the slang-riddled dialect of bass fishermen that combines all that is good and all that is bad about fish, fishermen, and fishing. The word stirs an onrush of thoughts and images so basic to the soul of the angler that

P R O   T I P S

The higher the sun climbs, the deeper you should fish.

BASS WAITING IN AMBUSH

During the summer, bass (below and facing page) wait hidden in ambush and move only a foot or less to capture their quarry. They will often strike a heavy flipping-style jig or Texas-rigged worm as it falls.

they could be characterized as nothing less than instinct. That word is "LUNKER!" Deep down inside, where love of the sport resides, most of us simply yearn to catch that lunker of a lifetime.

The lunker is a wise fish. It's seasoned. Savvy. In comparison to other fish, bass are endowed with some remarkable traits. Like humans, they see in color. Look a bass straight in the face, and you'll see high-set eyes and a mouth oriented upward toward the water's surface. This is the face that has launched a hundred thousand boats, designed and named just for bass. And every season those bass boats get more sophisticated and faster and sprout more high-tech instruments. Just like the skills in a predator's inventory, these boats are for perfecting an edge; they are all aimed at hunting one particular prey.

The water below the bass boat filters out virtually all colors within thirty feet of depth. The bass's color vision and upward eye and mouth orientation tell us they are

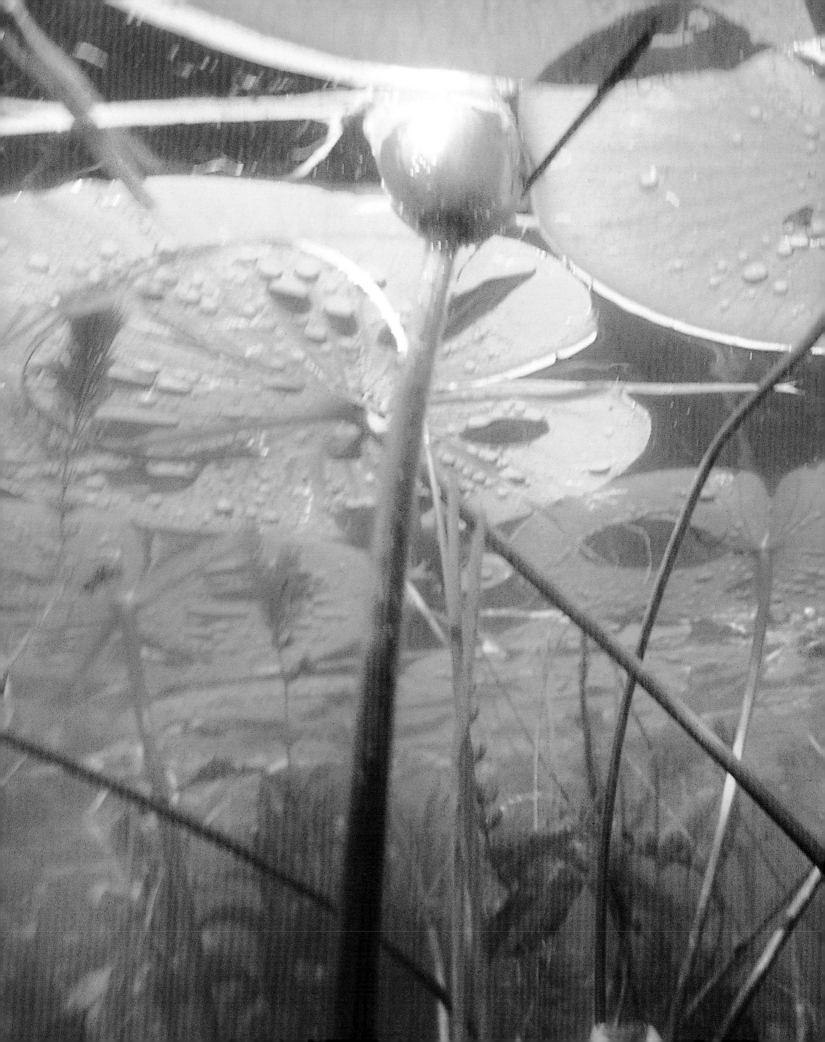

best suited to hunting their quarry in color-rich, brightly lit, shallow water and toward or actually on the surface. The broad, stocky body is highly maneuverable and capable of explosive bursts of speed, although it can't sustain that speed for any length of time. Like another species of predator—the big jungle cats—bass are built for quick kills. You can sometimes see them ripping through the surface, driving frenzied schools of baitfish into the air like the sparks of an arc welder.

The bigmouth is one of nature's favorite designs. Dozens of species of grouper cruising the oceans are indistinguishable in proportion from the largemouth bass. The design must be virtually perfect, because they look like clones of one another; yet they range in size from tiny reef grouper to the behemoth Warsaw, which can reach almost eight hundred pounds. It is also proof that the ultimate size of the bass is constrained only by the limitations of its environment.

Many species, including humans, require years, perhaps a quarter of their lifetime, to mature physically. Upon reaching maturity, growth ceases, the bones harden, and the natural process of aging begins. Although various restraints may limit the growth of a bass to perhaps two pounds a year, that development never ceases throughout their ten- to twenty-year life span. The ultimate size of a lunker is determined mostly by how much the fish eats balanced against how much energy it must expend in acquiring that food. The secret to superior growth within the species, then, is to achieve a small advantage and maintain that edge over the long haul. That edge could lie in camouflage, terrain, or tactics. Even more than most successful predators, bass are amazingly adaptable in each area.

Camouflage is one of the advantages bass have over other fish. Color cells in its skin allow the bass to change from tawny gold to leopard-spotted to tiger-striped in a matter of seconds. The patterned coats of the big cats enable each of them to succeed in a particular setting.

LUNKER

Of all the black bass, largemouth grow to the biggest sizes. Unlike the more muscular smallmouth or spotted bass, these fish prefer water with little or no movement. By lying in ambush in calm conditions, largemouth expend far less energy than their cousins, who must maintain their hunting position in a current.

The bold stripes of the tiger break up its form, making it virtually invisible in reed patches and tall grasses. The spotted coat of a leopard blends to eloquent perfection in the dappled light of the deepest jungle, and the tawny coat of a lioness is best suited to stalking herding animals at low light on savannahs and open plains. But the lunker bass can adapt to many environments. Buoyant and weightless in its watery home, the bass can effortlessly position itself in any plane and focus the full fury and energy of its sudden attack in the most advantageous direction. Unencumbered by the sound of footsteps, a lunker bass can outstalk the stealthiest of the big cats. And unlike land animals, the older a bass gets, the bigger and more capable it becomes. As a predator, the bass is in a class by itself, and because it reaches its peak at the end of its life, the best is always yet to come. ◀

—*Doug Hannon*

PREDATOR AND PREY

2 3

"He came straight at us *faster* than I could reel, *jumped,* and spit the lure right into the *boat.*"

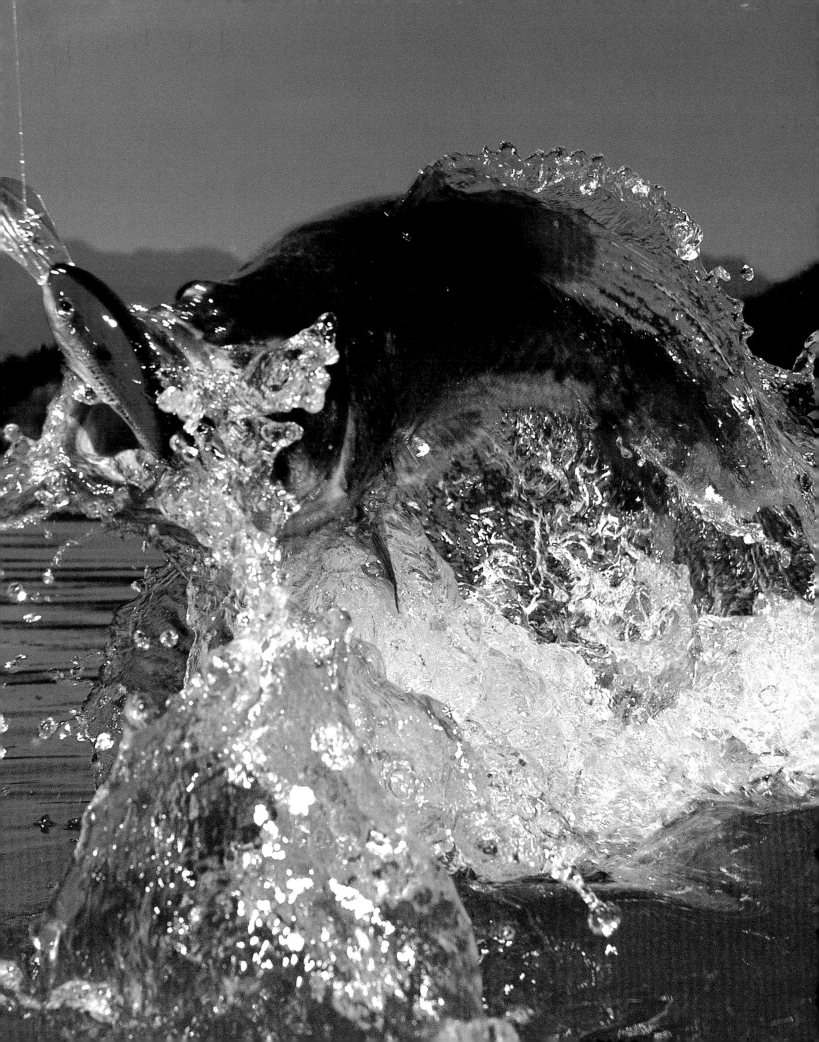

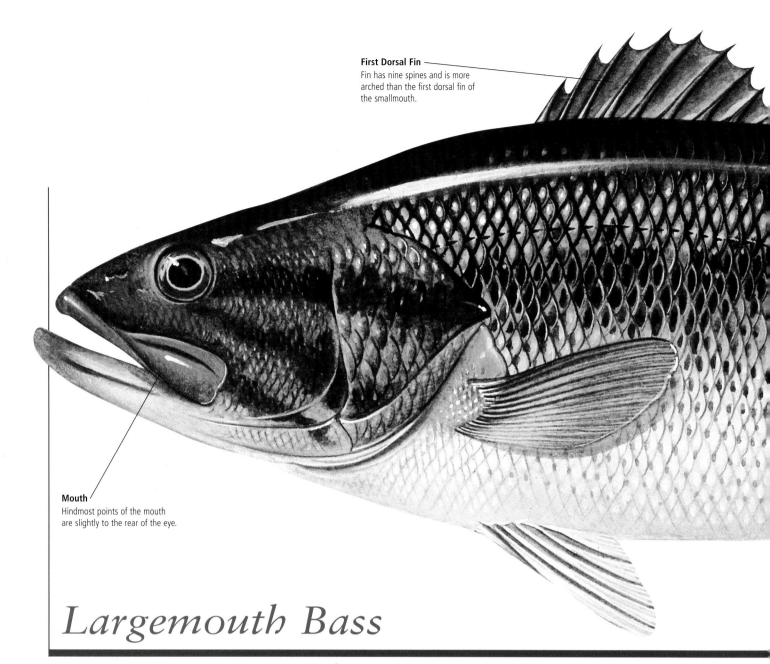

First Dorsal Fin
Fin has nine spines and is more arched than the first dorsal fin of the smallmouth.

Mouth
Hindmost points of the mouth are slightly to the rear of the eye.

Largemouth Bass

AMAZING ADAPTABILITY

On a typical summer day, largemouth can develop successful forage patterns in a wide range of habitats. Bass have adapted to a variety of forage types, which allows them to hunt crayfish on deep rocks, shad or trout in open water, minnows in the shallows, and even frogs, rodents, and smaller birds in the slop.

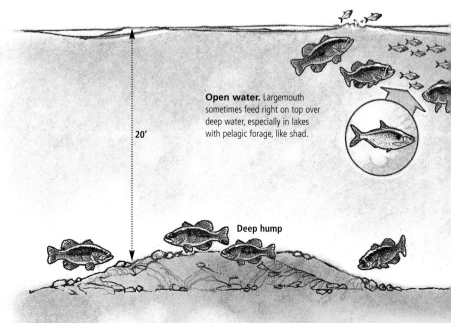

Open water. Largemouth sometimes feed right on top over deep water, especially in lakes with pelagic forage, like shad.

20'

Deep hump

Second Dorsal Fin
Fin has soft rays, not spines, and is almost separated from the first dorsal fin.

Flank Color
Flanks vary in color, according to water clarity and weed growth (this also applies to small-mouth).

Anal Fin
Fin is supported mostly by soft rays, but there are three short spines at the front end.

Slop. Some bass position here all summer.

Deep zone. Bass like the cover of rock piles on the lip of a secondary break.

15'

Shallow zone. Areas where a variety of weed types come together to create various edges make good hunting grounds for bass.

Deep weed edge. Areas where quick kills can be made of passing prey will attract bass.

DAWN SPLAYS ITS fingers across a clear sky. From underwater, the sun rises behind a green curtain. The visible world is about the size of a living room, with green drapes. Flooded with the diffuse, verdant light, it seems calm, benign, soothingly quiet. Small children sometimes swim here. But lurking behind the curtains is a deadly predator.

Predation, whether it means killing something to eat or being preyed upon, is the moment-to-moment concern of almost every creature on the planet except humans. So it's easy for us to forget how primal that dim world beneath the boat can be.

Largemouth Eggs in Weeds
Largemouth clear nests in weeds or, more often, scoop them with their tails in soft substrates like sand or loam. Eggs are ejected by the female, then fertilized by the male.

For the first several years of its life, a bass is a potential meal for predators of every shape, style, and species. Insects, turtles, birds, raccoons, bears, and, of course, other fish are the primary threats to young bass as they desperately struggle to survive, eat, and grow. Most will perish. In fact, less than one percent of all bass fry eventually reach adulthood, even though survival of the fittest is a game for which the black bass are well suited. That's how dangerous the underwater world is when you're born a fish.

Actually, the average nest in North America produces only about two adult bass—just

enough recruitment to replace the parents, even though female largemouth lay between seven thousand and eighty thousand eggs per pound of body weight. This means a five-pound female could lay as many as four hundred thousand eggs!

Some environments eventually produce more adults from each spawning endeavor, but others are considerably harsher. In some lakes, where there is uncommon pressure from cormorants or larger predatory fish, like muskies, or any of a thousand other potential threats, the bass population is barely able to replace itself each year through spawning. This can be especially true in

lakes where there are significant changes to shoreline areas. Developers installing seawalls, homeowners cleaning out debris and deadfall, people spraying herbicides, and other regrettable lakefront practices reduce the spawning habitat for bass by thousands of acres per year in this country.

In spite of all the obstacles to their survival, largemouth are thriving in reservoirs, rivers, ponds, lakes, and streams from southern Canada to central Mexico. Already well dispersed throughout their natural range, they have been stocked in thousands of other waterways. Their aggressive nature and extreme adaptability make these fish very successful transplants and wildly popular with anglers. As a result, although native only to North America, largemouth are now being stocked throughout the world from Europe and Africa to Japan and South America.

Waiting in the Shade
Bass hover under big schools of shad, shiners, trout, and other forage fish far from shore during summer. A soft-plastic jerkbait twitched through the school of bait screams, "Injured fish!"

THE WORLD OF THE
Largemouth Bass

"This is the *face* that launched a hundred thousand *boats.*"

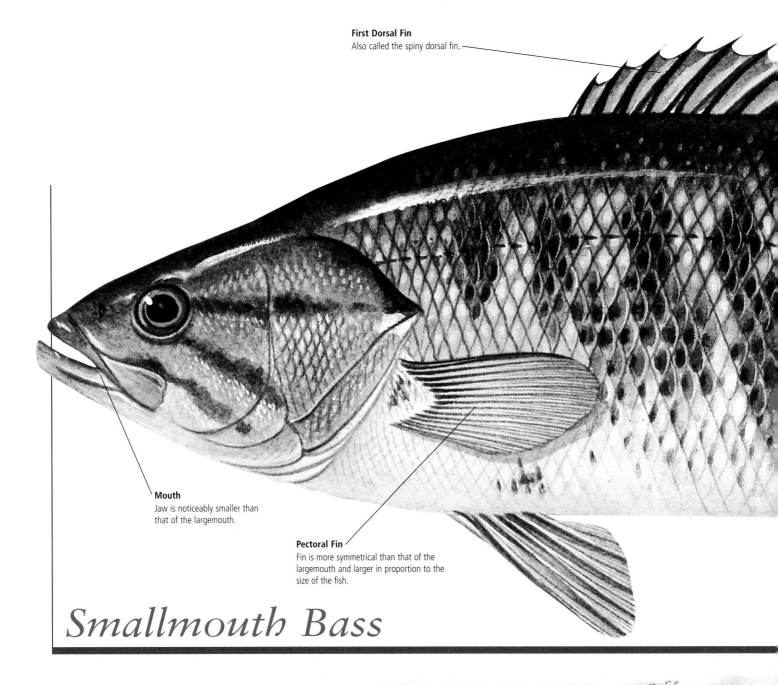

First Dorsal Fin
Also called the spiny dorsal fin.

Mouth
Jaw is noticeably smaller than
that of the largemouth.

Pectoral Fin
Fin is more symmetrical than that of the
largemouth and larger in proportion to the
size of the fish.

Smallmouth Bass

CURRENT SWIMMERS

River smallmouth are current swimmers, and
generally more active than largemouth because of
their habitats in moving water. Like the largemouth,
they prefer transitions in the underwater terrain,
and will face upstream while lying hidden behind
boulders, wood cover, and other current breaks.
In an active pattern, they often wait in fairly shallow
water just upstream of current eddies, and prefer
deeper pools when less active.

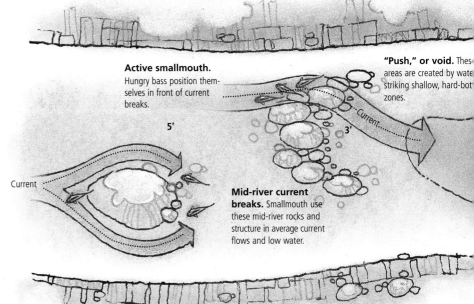

Active smallmouth.
Hungry bass position themselves in front of current
breaks.

5′

Current

"Push," or void. These
areas are created by water
striking shallow, hard-bot-
tom zones.

Current

3′

**Mid-river current
breaks.** Smallmouth use
these mid-river rocks and
structure in average current
flows and low water.

Second Dorsal Fin
Unlike the largemouth, the smallmouth's second dorsal fin is joined to the first.

Color
Smallmouth has a more bronze coloration than the largemouth, with side markings like vertical bars.

Anal Fin
Fin is more rounded than that of the largemouth.

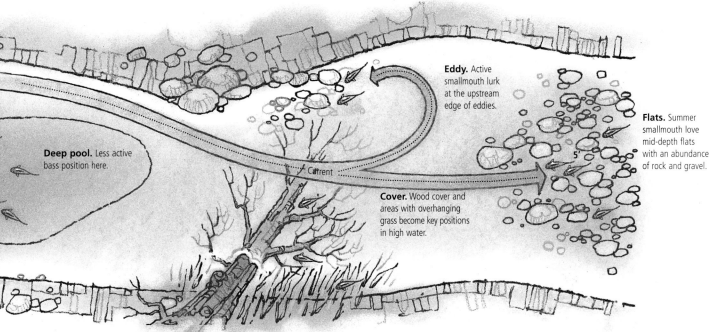

Eddy. Active smallmouth lurk at the upstream edge of eddies.

Flats. Summer smallmouth love mid-depth flats with an abundance of rock and gravel.

Deep pool. Less active bass position here.

Current

5′

Cover. Wood cover and areas with overhanging grass become key positions in high water.

THE ORIGINAL RANGE of smallmouth bass encompassed the watersheds of the Great Lakes, the Ohio River, and the Mississippi River. Now they flourish from the rocky lakes of the Canadian Shield south to Alabama and from Maine to the Columbia River. Even Vancouver Island, surrounded by the Pacific Ocean, is home to smallmouth bass.

Their spread throughout this expansive range is the result of careful planning in some instances and of "bucket biologists" in others. In Ontario, for instance, camp cooks hauled smallmouth to lakes and streams by the barrelful. This gave them easier access to fish they could catch to feed the lumberjacks.

Smallmouth are basically shallow-water fish that prowl rocky shorelines, reefs, weed beds, and nearby open water in

search of prey. Renowned for being hard-nosed fighters, they are also homebodies; that is, they may not range far to find suitable habitat for the season. For example, they may set up shop in a small lake, when deeper wintering areas lie close to suitable shallow spawning areas, and their summer habitat lies in between. In the Great Lakes, however, they may winter five miles or more from spawning sites. The distances between seasonal habitats tend to be larger in larger bodies of water.

In lakes, smallmouth typically winter forty to fifty feet deep on the edges of basin flats that adjoin big points and bars extending from shallow shoreline areas out to deep water.

River smallmouth prefer pools and holes at least twenty feet deep. When the water warms to 46°F, they wander out toward their spawning habitat. Most will spawn in water temperatures of 60°F to 64°F on sand or gravel, usually near boulders, stickups, logs, or fallen trees. Males scoop out nests with their tails and stay to protect the eggs and hatchlings. This ensures the survival of many young but tires and debilitates the males, leaving them vulnerable to predators.

During summer, smallmouth may leave the shallow reefs and shorelines to follow big pods of bait over open water. It's common to find them suspended twenty feet down over depths of sixty to one hundred feet in sprawling

reservoirs and natural lakes. But the next day they'll be back in a shallow habitat, making anglers think that the fish "just weren't biting yesterday."

Watching smallmouth relate to other fish in a tank is enlightening. An adult can herd groups of bigger largemouths and walleye into a corner and keep them corralled for weeks. And woe to the one that tries to move. The smallmouth will repeatedly nudge it back into its place. They will attack much larger muskies and pike that wander near their spawning beds. It's easy to admire that spirit.

And spirit they have. Hooked smallmouth can fly out of the water up to five times the length of their bodies. They have more muscle than largemouth, so smaller specimens often weigh more and pull harder. Brown bass, smalljaws, bronzebacks, smallies, thumb-breakers—no matter what you call them, few fish pull so hard for so long as smallmouth bass.

High Flyers
Highly active smallmouth simply can't resist crankbaits, and they are bound to fly when hooked.

THE WORLD OF THE
Smallmouth Bass

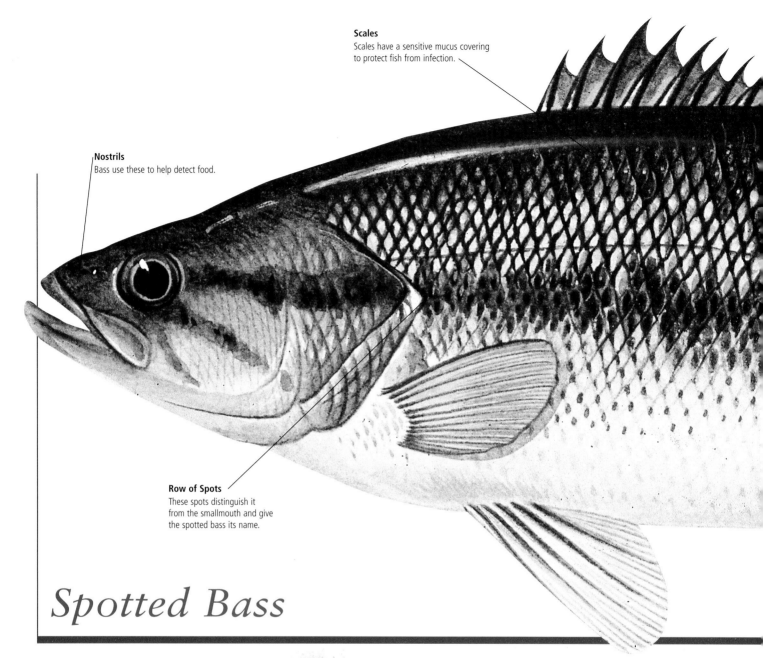

Scales
Scales have a sensitive mucus covering
to protect fish from infection.

Nostrils
Bass use these to help detect food.

Row of Spots
These spots distinguish it
from the smallmouth and give
the spotted bass its name.

Spotted Bass

A NICHE OF THEIR OWN

Spotted bass occupy a niche between the largemouth
and smallmouth. They generally congregate in areas
with more current than largemouth prefer, but in warmer
water temperatures and with less water movement
than smallmouth like. Their diet varies as they mature,
moving from zooplankton to insects, and finally to
smaller fish and crayfish. Since they will spawn at a
variety of depths, they are especially suited to reservoirs
with fluctuating water levels. Steeply sloping banks,
especially areas with gravel, silt, or organic matter on the
bottom, will be likely places to look for these fish.

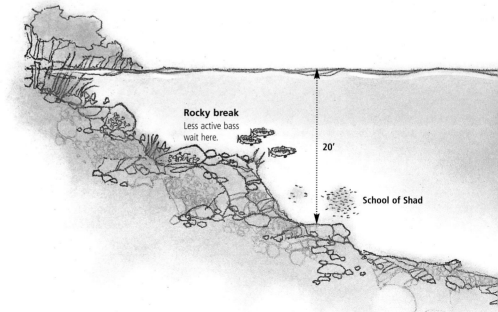

Rocky break
Less active bass
wait here.

20′

School of Shad

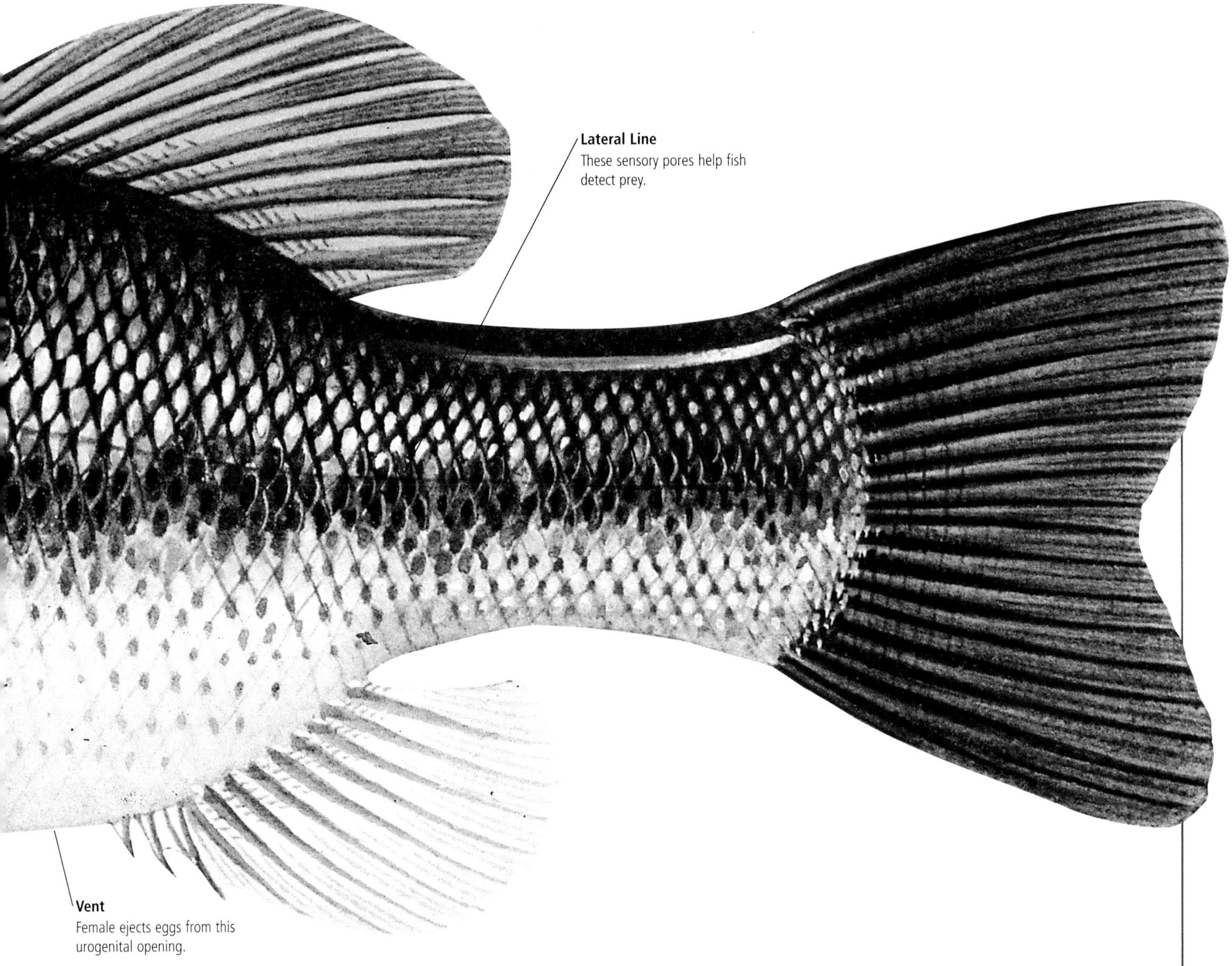

Lateral Line
These sensory pores help fish detect prey.

Vent
Female ejects eggs from this urogenital opening.

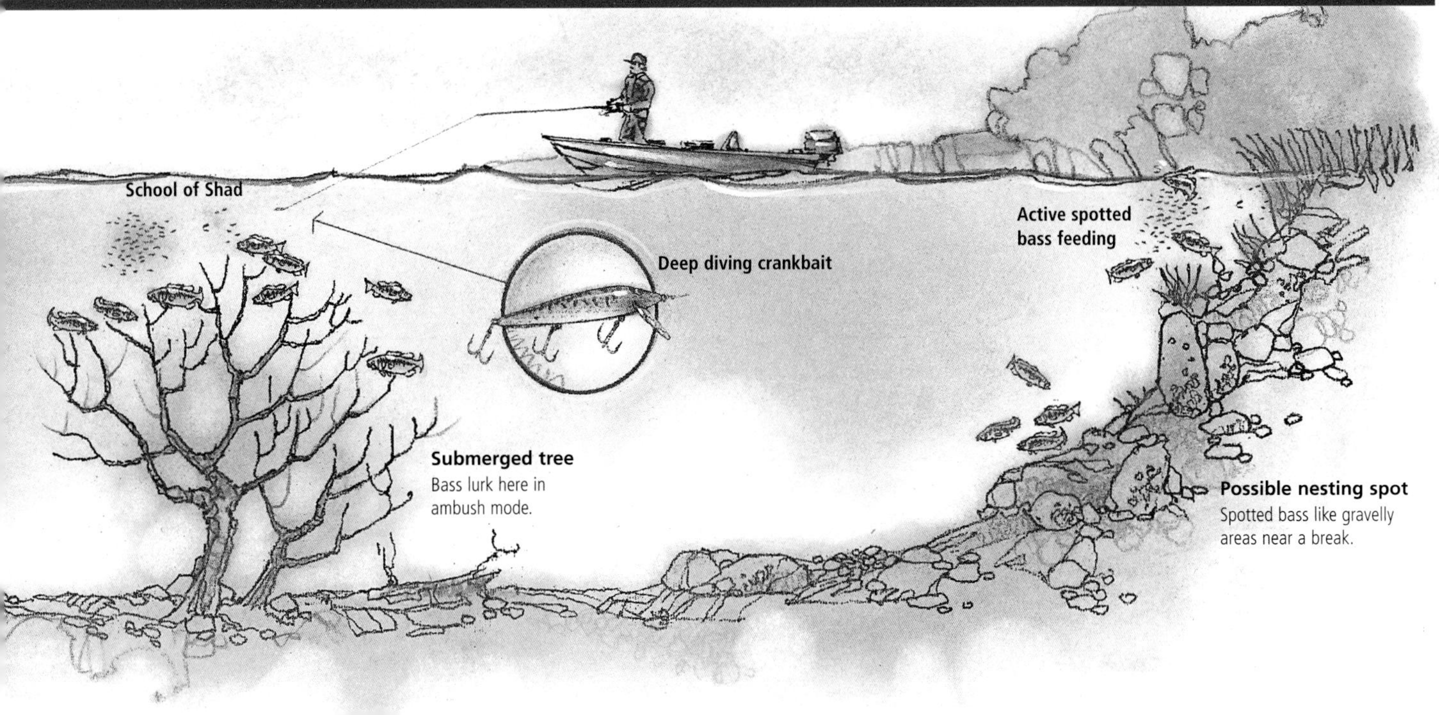

School of Shad

Deep diving crankbait

Active spotted bass feeding

Submerged tree
Bass lurk here in ambush mode.

Possible nesting spot
Spotted bass like gravelly areas near a break.

EACH SEASON OF her twelve- to fifteen-year lifetime, a female bass will lay thousands of eggs in order to ensure a small number mature to carry on the line. A healthy lake of some two thousand acres can sustain a population of four thousand to six thousand spawning-age bass, with no more than three hundred over five pounds. Now, keep in mind what the odds are of even one of these millions of eggs surviving to maturity. Perhaps only one in eleven nests has even one egg hatch and is not simply abandoned by the protective male to swarms of predators like bluegills, minnows, or other panfish. Even if he is successful in guarding some of the eggs for the four to seven days until they hatch, he must then protect the undisciplined cloud of baby fry for up to six weeks until they reach about an inch in length and disperse into heavy cover to fend for themselves.

Once the parental duties have been fulfilled, and for the remainder of the spring, summer, and fall, the young inhabit a thick, protective cover of weed beds or whatever else they can find. It is here they learn the exclusionary nature of predation: they must temper the want-everything mentality of youth and learn, bite by bite, to exclude things they cannot have from their diet. For the baby bass, these might be creatures as large as or even larger than themselves, things that do not seem to fear or react to them with flight, things with bright yellow and black warning colors or sharp fin spines, or those that are so fast the young ones never seem to be able to catch them. The few fingerlings that survive this passage will heed the warm promise of summer and leave the sheltered shallows with an imprinted selection of the options necessary to thrive and grow.

It is the job of our lunker bass to learn the prime feeding spots and strategies in this area. She must be quick to establish and sustain dominance and feeding superiority in the niche of her size group, moving on as soon as possible to the next niche. The metabolic demand, feeding

activity, and growth rate of the bass peak at a water temperature of 78°F to 82°F. The biggest fish will be those that are able to exploit fully the few months of summer's peak window and make the most efficient use of the lesser opportunities offered during the other three seasons.

As the sun moves farther north, the nights turn chilly, and summer fades into fall, our aspiring trophy fish must now master another season. The focus of activity during fall is toward deeper water. She must pick the most direct migration route possible that also provides a lavishly abundant food supply along the way. Fish now gather in schools and move out to the deepest margins of weed beds, tree lines, or other submerged cover until they find the points and projections that lead to the deep water closest to bait-holding cover, the ideal winter quarters.

Once the fall migration is complete, winter is a time of rest. While many of the world's living things require more food to maintain body heat during the cold, the bass's cold-blooded

Never try to scoop the fish up. Instead, gently lead it over to the waiting net. Out of the water, the bass's body weight can tear a hook free.

metabolism reduces its demand for food and oxygen to near nil by the time the water reaches the low forties. Even with their senses dulled, those few destined to reach lunker proportions maintain an edge, however slight, in energy and spirit that gradually separates them from the pack. They make forays closer to the surface on sunny days or during Indian summers. With physiological demand for food so low, any small extra morsels go a long way toward providing reserve sustenance. Giant bass seem to maintain the highest level of

activity, even when the lake is covered with ice and most of the warm-water fish are in hibernation. As a result, the largest bass ever recorded in Massachusetts— or, for that matter, in any other northern state—was an amazing specimen weighing 15.5 pounds, caught on Sampson Pond by an ice fisherman.

If you're hardy enough to chase big bass through the winter months, you'll do best when you remember the winter fishing watchwords, "deep and steep." Most bass are found on banks with a slope greater than forty-five degrees. They can go for weeks this time of year without any food and then eat only very small morsels. Most of their movements within the water column are vertical rather than horizontal. You will be most likely to find bass if you concentrate on those steep drop-offs located in

twenty to forty feet of water on the points around creek mouths and near bends in the main lake channel. The best offerings should include small, heavy lures fished vertically on light line. A small silver spoon fished yo-yo style straight under the boat just might angle you a firsthand encounter with that winter

lunker before she returns in early spring, heavy with eggs, to that warm northern cove where she hatched and found a way to survive so many seasons ago.

Preparing the Nest
Nesting bass like to create their beds near vertical cover, which provides security from some predators.

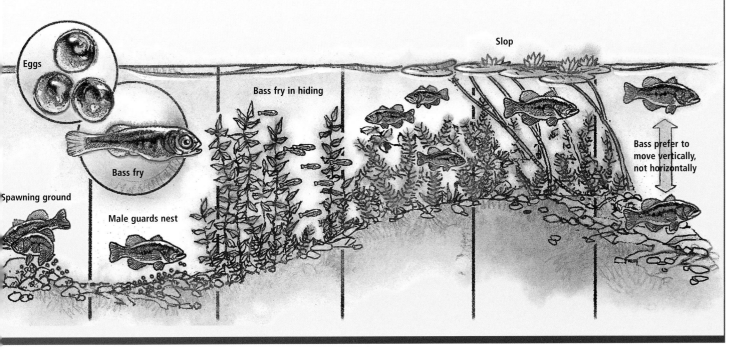

Eggs

Spawning ground

Bass fry

Male guards nest

Bass fry in hiding

Slop

Bass prefer to move vertically, not horizontally

"I knew he was *down there,*
as well hidden as stars on a sunny day."

Ambush
A bass approaches its prey from the side out of its ambush position.

Quick Strike
The first objective is to stun or kill the prey.

An Easy Meal
Once the prey is helpless, the bass will turn it and take it in headfirst.

Down the Hatch
This way the spines on the dorsal fin lie down, and the scales slide past the bass's gullet without flaring or lodging.

THE WORLD OF BASS
How Bass Feed

*"She ran in two wide circles,
then* **jumped,**
as if to get a look at me."

The Old Game

In the dusty cigar box of my childhood memories linger: the creak of oarlocks over quiet water; cane poles poised along the gunwales with the butts secured underfoot; long tips that bobbed to the rhythmic cadence of the boat, a wooden hull with bench seats. Water bled through chipped caulk as the boat nosed slowly around thickets of weed beds and forests of reeds. Our dark lines trailed off into the morning mist. The tips of our poles bowed to the pull of a minnow harness behind a light egg-sinker rig. . .

These were the unending days of boyhood summers. My cousin would row steadily to an ancient rhythm, his eyes riveted on the tips of the poles. Instinct often re-created the familiar surge-and-pause rowing rhythm that seldom failed to trigger the green boil of a bass behind the boat. The cane would creak, thrash, and quickly double into a dangerous arc as a big bass snatched the bait and pulled away toward safety. "Grab it!" we'd holler.

Sometimes we missed and the pole went overboard. It would float, bobbing and turning with mesmerizing purpose. Sometimes the bass erupted, shaking its head and flinging spray in an effort to throw the hook. Sometimes it played ostrich and buried its head in the weeds. Pushing one oar and pulling the other, we turned the boat, the cadence suddenly hurried by a jolt of adrenaline.

In later years we abandoned live-bait rigs for something new and deadly called the Rapala, as our old cane poles gave way to glass and, eventually, graphite rods. The Rapala would bob to the surface, then, with two strong strokes of the oars, shimmy down to four feet or so. Sometimes bass would explode through the surface film for the resting minnowbait. Sometimes they slashed at the lure as it paused at running depth. In May, when prespawn bass were gathering shallow in my home state of Michigan, a Rapala alternately twitching and resting on the surface often triggered astonishing watery explosions.

In those days, we thought the proliferation of surface lures, plastics, and crankbaits designed for bass must surely have reached the saturation point. We felt we had more choices than we needed. A peek into one of today's major fishing catalogs would have precipitated a severe case of future shock. Imagine what such a peek might do to the psyche of a bass fisherman from the nineteenth century or a cave dweller living in the twilight of the Ice Age.

Long before the trout-mad Europeans arrived, and well before the most recent Ice Age, bass were haunting the open expanses and vegetated shallows of American rivers and lakes. When the last glacier of that epoch finally dragged its algid, shrinking

SMALLMOUTH BAIT

Even before the sun warms the water, the fishing can be hot. Minnowbaits can be deadly for shallow smallmouth in spring when they're twitched on the surface, snapped and jerked along just beneath the surface, or retrieved slowly and steadily.

fingers back into the Arctic ten thousand years ago, members of the bass family (*Micropterus salmoides*) began wending their way north again through watercourses gouged into the earth by two-mile-high walls of ice. They migrated up rivers of melt and runoff. In the following millennia, bass acclimated to a wide range of habitats throughout eastern North America, which is their only ancestral home. When Europeans first settled here, black bass were naturally distributed from what is today northern Mexico to southern Canada and from the Mississippi River to the Atlantic Ocean. During those near-forgotten centuries, they were a summer staple for eastern Native Americans, because bass stay shallow, making them easier to find and trap or spear throughout the warm months when other big fish go deep. So a cave wall probably served as the canvas for the world's earliest artistic endeavors featuring black bass.

The first serious written dissertation on black bass appeared in 1881, with the publication of *The Book of Black Bass*, by Dr. James Alexander Henshall. "The Black Bass is wholly unknown in the Old World except where recently introduced, and exists naturally only in America," he wrote. "No doubt the Black Bass is the appointed successor to the Lordly Trout [and] will eventually become the leading game fish in America, [at least that] is my oft-expressed opinion and firm belief." That was a bold prediction 120 years ago, when the "Lordly Trout" ruled the hearts of anglers throughout Western civilization. It was inaccurate only in the sense that it fell far short of predicting just how high the popularity of bass would rocket in the century to come.

Today bass are found in every state except Alaska and have been distributed across the globe. The largemouth bass has become, by every statistical and spiritual gauge employed, America's fish. Part of its newfound popularity is directly attributable to the creation of hundreds of reservoirs throughout the South in the mid-twentieth century, where natural lakes are

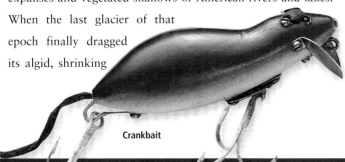

Crankbait

rare. Those reservoirs are now home to several species of bass that thrive in great numbers and reach prodigious (sometimes preposterous) sizes. Even more preposterous are the Florida-strain largemouth introduced into the Southwest. Reservoirs in California, for instance, occasionally produce largemouth in the twenty-pound range.

Jigging Spoons

But the lion's share of this latent notoriety is due to tournament angling, which skyrocketed in popularity during the late 1960s and early 1970s, eventually granting "ol' bucketmouth" the momentum to overtake stream trout in the hearts of American anglers. America loves competition and homegrown resources; by these standards, the bass family is more American than apple pie, predating it by some several thousand years.

The *Micropterus* family boasts seven members in North America (largemouth, smallmouth, spotted, shoal, Suwannee, Coosa, and Guadalupe). Though they all look fairly similar, the size potential, coloration, and morphology vary a bit from group to group. The world-record largemouth bass, for instance, is the famous 22-pound 4-ounce giant wrestled out of Montgomery Lake, Georgia, by George Perry back in 1932, while the world-record Guadalupe bass stands at 3 pounds 11 ounces. A wide variety of lures, baits, and presentations can be used to catch any of the black bass. In

MORNING CATCH

In the early morning mist, smallmouth prowl through the tranquil waters gracing some of North America's most pristine wilderness areas. The fight they put up can provide a wake-up call more bracing, and far more memorable, than the strongest cup of coffee.

fact, no other species of fish worldwide has inspired nearly so many lure types or styles. That so many varied shapes, sizes, colors, textures, and actions appeal to bass is testament to their voracity and adaptability.

Artificial baits in Henshall's day were confined to flies, "spoon baits" (which included forerunners of both contemporary spoons and straight-shafted spinners), and artificial minnows. Before the turn of the century, minnow plugs were crafted of metal, rubber, or glass; styled into shapes resembling small fish; and armed with one or two small treble hooks. In the many decades since, bass lures have blinked in and out of existence with clockwork regularity, leaving modern antique hunters with a long, amusing, and colorful list of collectibles. Lucky Louie. Gee Wiz Frog. Bag-O-Mad. Glutton Dibbler. Stubby's Hydroplug. The Scandinavian Sockaroo. Lucid-Lure. Dowegiac Minnow. The P&K Whirl-A-Way. Bass-Oreno. Tin Liz. Rush Tango. Jitterbug. Not to mention Opie of Mayberry's infamous Golly Whomper.

The first lines used by bass fishermen were made of cotton, linen, or silk and either braided or twisted into a ponderous string that needed to be dried from time to time during a day's fishing. As for early methodology, Henshall discussed two basic means: fly-fishing and "minnow tackle," which employed ash and lancewood rods that were eight to nine feet long. The "multiplying reels," early forerunners of

today's casting reels, were designed with free-running spools that required constant thumb pressure during a cast to avoid horrific and spectacular bird's nests. About the time Henshall penned his definitive work, a young man named Fred Henkel was learning how to fish. "The very first equipment I had was a birch pole," Henkel wrote in a letter to Lou Eppinger, Inc., regarding his first purchase of the now-famous Dardevle spoon. "My dad cut it for me. A piece of wrapping string and a penny's worth of ring hooks and a cork from an old bottle completed the necessary outfit. It wasn't so long, but it seemed like ages before we graduated from the birch pole class to the long bamboo stage. We used to buy them at the store for fifteen cents. I always picked out the longest one in the bunch; it didn't cost any more.

Antique Ambassador Reel

Rocks and wood retain the sun's warmth longer, so in early spring, these are the places to look first.

"We felt pretty smart with our store poles, using sunfish belly to skitter for bass. Half of the time the bass would land up in a tree with the tip of the pole and the line all tangled galley-west."

Next time you're on the water, take a close look at the graphite rod and ball-bearing reel with infinite antireverse in your hands and be thankful for small favors. Modern bass rods and reels are made with space age materials. Today's lines are stronger and produce longer casts than those of yesterday. Lures are more lifelike and designed with casting distance, depth range, texture, flash, sound, and vibration variables—you name it.

In defiance, one August day I observed the old tradition of live bait on a hook along a break, looking for river smallmouth without finding many. I figured they had left the area since my last visit, until six simultaneous eruptions shattered the shadowy calm beneath an oak tree, tight to the bank. Carp? I slipped over that way and dropped anchor softly, just beneath the afternoon shadow of the towering trees.

I reached for the rod with a popper attached. It's an old game. Check the hooks. Test the knot. Check the wind. Make a sidearm cast under the overhang. Stop the lure over the water. Bring it down soft. Let it drift. Manage the line. Wait. Snap the rod tip down. The surface lure popped, bobbed, stilled itself, and drifted across the interface between four worlds: peace and calamity, air and water. Birdsong and shadow surrounded the moment. I twitched the rod and the bait vibrated softly.

Few things in nature are less predictable than a surface strike from a black bass. Images of the event are an American icon, adorning cereal boxes, billboards, and cigarette lighters from coast to coast. With active bass around, a surface bait bobbing in the chop is high drama. This is why cabin fever exists. All winter where I live, while the wind whistles and redistributes the snowy landscape, I find myself launching rowboats in my mind's eye with increasing regularity as spring approaches.

Sitting in my office, I picture lily pads lifting and waving in the wind on a distant lake or beds of eelgrass floating in the August currents of the Mississippi River outside my window. Such pastoral daydreams inevitably fall prey to the barbarity of a rude but accommodating creature with a large, indiscriminate maw. Before long, the imaginary bass is hooked. It rises over the misty surface and flops wildly, desperately back into that mysterious medium that captured us as children. Water. Home of crawdads and fish and other creatures from a world that we can only visit for a few moments at a time, though our imaginations will never leave it. Home of those marvelous, impossible mysteries our fathers hunted and called "bronzebacks," "bucketmouths," or, simply, "black bass."

—Matt Straw

MODERN BASS FISHING began in a day when people had no specific target species in mind. Mostly, fishermen were looking for dinner. That, and for a good day on the water, alive to the possibility of each moment but relaxed and forgetful of all other cares in the sunlight of a summer's day. Rods were Tonkin bamboo, lines were braided silk, spoons were sterling silver, and reels were jewel-bearing microwinches, handmade by eccentric watchmakers.

Shuttle forward to the 1960s, and suddenly the world discovered bass fishing. The pastime changed to a competitive

Addictive Qualities
Surface lures should come with a warning label: "Beware. Use of these lures has been known to be habit-forming."

spectator sport, collapsed in on itself, and then exploded. What emerged had no resemblance to its previous form. Lures evolved, ranging from artfully crafted wooden replicas of baitfish to ostentatious, fluorescent-hued hunks of rattling acrylic; gaudy silicone-skirted creations with giant water-frothing blades; and Steuben-clear, stained-glass-colored, soft plastic anomalies that resembled microbes you might see when looking at pond water through a microscope.

Much to everyone's astonishment, the bass could not seem to get enough of these

creatures. What type of natural food did these outlandish aquatic confections represent to the fish? Airline food, perhaps. It doesn't look like anything you would eat, but you eat it anyway, and in front of strangers. Somehow, it seemed that this fish was impossible to offend, and that just made America fall even more in love with it.

Tournament fishing exploded onto the late 1960s scene like some aquatic Age of Aquarius and, overnight, drove the industry through an era of development and commercialization that would be considered unprecedented in

any sport. Rods quickly evolved from fiberglass to carbon fiber and beyond, to blends of boron, titanium, and even Kevlar. Reels became high-tech, with complex rare-earth magnetic antibacklash systems and exotic alloys. Every aspect of the sport followed suit. Before long, the boats became even more garish than the lures and, with their newly designed, giant outboard motors, were streaking across the water at speeds approaching ninety mph.

We owe all of this to the promotion and marketing of bass fishing, and it has showed no signs of abatement. This very weekend on any U. S. Army Corps of Engineers reservoir you will find more sonar pinging from the transducers of bass boats than a World War II North Atlantic convoy. In spite of it all, the single biggest dream of the average bass angler is to go out today and catch, not a tournament-winning creel, but the "lunker of a lifetime."

Dreams of Giant Bass
In the days of wooden boats and fedoras, tackle was carried in tin boxes, and line was made of braided Dacron, but the dreams were the same.

Era of the Bass

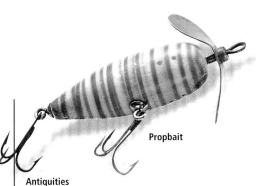

Propbait

Antiquities

Not long ago, bass in many waters had seen very few plugs and lures, because getting to them required rowing, and anglers had less reliable information to guide them than do fishermen of today.

The Old-fashioned Way

The old reels were usually direct drive, but even the geared models like the one below had no anti-reverse mechanism. Anglers who experienced a hard hit by a bass called these reels "knucklebusters."

A Simpler Time

Old lures and like these in the tackle box above hark back to a simpler time, when a soda was five cents and a round of golf cost fifty cents—on weekends!

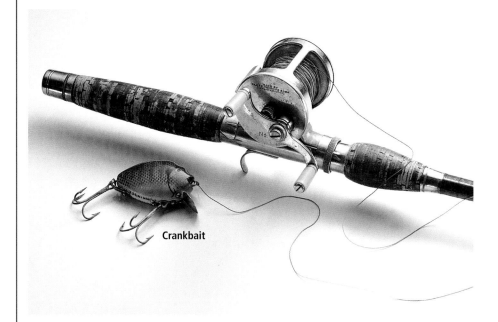

Crankbait

GOLDEN MEMORIES
Antique Fishing Gear

Hand-painted Lures
Old lures were usually made of cedar or basswood, and many were hand-turned on a lathe.

BASS RELY ON several senses to capture prey. When an active, hungry bass searches for food, the first sense to come into play could be touch. Along the midsection of most fish, a series of pores that detect low-level vibrations completes a tactile system called the lateral line. Through this line, bass can feel vibrations below hearing level, those in the frequency range of one to two hundred cycles per second. Often a bass can feel the distress signals of a wounded or dying minnow long before it sees or hears the prey.

Hearing is the next sense that comes into play. As our hungry, active predator approaches the source of the vibration, it begins to hear any struggles the prey makes that cause vibrations in the frequency range of one hundred to thirteen thousand cycles per second. Of course, if the source of curiosity is a rattling crankbait instead of a wounded baitfish the bass would hear the bait first, or hear and feel it at the same time. In muddy or cloudy water, where visibility is reduced to less than a foot, the bass rely on their tactile and auditory senses. Without these tools they couldn't survive long periods of runoff and flooding.

As they approach prey in clearer water, sight becomes the principal targeting tool. Vision provides the surest way for bass to zero in on their prey and kill it. This seems to be the sense bass would prefer to rely on. Many biologists refer to bass as "sight feeders." Where waters are always cloudy and visibility is always bad, bass often manage to grow large by taking advantage of areas where visibility is best.

Bass have monocular vision (vision with one eye) on each side of their head and an expanding cone of binocular vision (where both eyes can focus on things) that extends forward immediately in front of their face. When bass perceive vibrations or see movement, they turn toward it to place it in that cone of binocular vision. This allows them to better compensate for the prey's evasive movements.

These fish also have a good sense of taste. Some observers would say that, given the photographic evidence, it far surpasses that of fishermen. But we're not talking about clothing style here—we're talking about the palate. When a bass grabs something, taste buds in its lips and mouth immediately determine if it's food. Bass are adept at spitting lures.

When active bass overtake their prey, they try to crush them. They can crush prey so quickly and thoroughly that bits of bone and blood often squirt out through the bass's gills. Actively feeding bass like to strike at the head of their prey, and this is why a Texas rig requires only one hook, right at the head or forward portion of the bait.

Less active bass tend to approach a potential meal very slowly and from the rear until they are very near, then try to suck it in. They do this by flaring open their gill plates, which quickly draws water and any potential food that lies suspended nearby into their mouth. This is what happens when a bass fisherman feels a mushy "tick" when using lighter plastic baits or jigs. Less active bass may not pursue the item further if they fail to suck it in immediately. This means that heavier jigs will often fail where lighter ones, with the hook placed closer to the tail, would succeed, especially when all the bass in the lake seem to be inactive or neutral about feeding. It is crucial for a fisherman to understand the activity level of the bass and then be able to select and rig lures accordingly.

Several factors, including weather, determine activity levels. When the barometric pressure rises or drops beyond a certain point, bass fishing ceases to be fantastic. A few fish are always biting, but a summer cold front will almost always turn off most bass. Fall cold fronts, on the other hand, actually seem to stimulate feeding at times, as if Mother Nature is prodding them to stock up on nutrients for that long, cold winter ahead.

THE WORLD OF BASS
Underwater Senses

Although they are terribly effective predators, bass are also scavengers. Recently killed baitfish lying on the bottom are fair game. Sometimes still-fishing with dead bait works better than actively fishing with lures. Bass rely on their sense of smell to locate dead minnows. They have two nostrils positioned directly above their mouth. These nostrils funnel water to olfactory organs, which, although much less well developed than those of a carp or a catfish, occasionally serve quite well for finding convenient meals that can't easily escape an ambush or fight back.

Bass are very adaptive, and forage on a variety of things, from birds to aquatic insects, mice, frogs, or minnows. But they feed mainly on whatever is most abundant and easiest to catch.

Active Feeders
When bass are intent on eating, they prefer to strike at the head of their prey. This is why a Texas rig generally has one hook, located at the forward position of the bait.

SWEAT THE DETAILS. Slide the last few feet of line through your fingers every few casts to feel for nicks and abrasions. If there's any question, cut it off and retie. Learn to sharpen hooks properly. Make sure the hooks on each lure are sharp. Examine your lure frequently and clean any gunk from the swivels and hardware as soon as it accumulates. You only get so many chances, so why not do what you can to ensure that everything will go right when the next one occurs?

BE OBSERVANT. If you see a swirl, cast to it. If you notice an increase in animal activity along the shoreline, or if the frogs seem particularly active in a lily pad bed, get busy and stay alert. Like the bass, animal behavior is influenced by factors that we may not recognize because we are too far removed from our primordial origins. Often, the whole food chain stirs from

the bottom up; increased activity anywhere in it could mean an impending surge in bass activity.

FISH DRY LAND. Whenever you look at a landscape, imagine it flooded. Try to visualize the paths the fish would follow as they move in that habitat. Where would they position themselves to gain an advantage? Picture yourself in a boat floating overhead, and try to figure out where you should be casting, based on what's visible above your imaginary waterline. This will help you guess where fish might be waiting for a meal and determine how to present a lure to those spots.

VISUALIZE ON THE WATER. Read the lay of the land, your depth sounder, and the information each cast gives you about the contours and conditions below. As you

fish, try to create a mental image of this corner of the bass's world. Picture your lure as it swims, sinks, or climbs over obstructions. Try to visualize where the lairs of the bass are. Then try to get your lure into those places and make it act particularly vulnerable when it's there.

WEAR GOOD POLARIZED GLASSES. You and the fish live in different worlds, and the more you know about his, the more successful you'll be. Depth sounders and topographic maps help, but their information is limited. A pair of polarized sunglasses lets you see a little farther and a little

more clearly into the water. In many cases, they let you see exactly what your lure does in response to your rod tip artistry and how fish react to those movements.

THINK COMBINATIONS AND INTERSECTIONS. A submerged log is a fine piece of cover and may hold a bass. The deep edge of a weed bed is a super breakline and will usually be attractive to bass. But if that log is lying across the edge of a weedline, you can bet the bass will use that spot along the weed edge and that log will be a good casting target. Where two forms of

GOOD HABITS
Catch More Fish

cover intersect, or where the edge of cover abuts good structure, is likely to be a good spot.

KEEP A LOG. The simple act of recording information forces you to analyze and compare it more than you otherwise would. It also helps you recognize patterns that might not be evident at first glance. It doesn't matter if the log is handwritten, recorded on your way home from the lake, or typed into a computer database once you're home, as long as it works for you.

BE A WEATHER FORECASTER. When it comes to weather, trends are more important than current conditions. Enter the weather conditions into your log every day, not just on the days you fish. If your entry says the fish did such-and-such on a 74°F cloudy day in July, you're not going to remember three years later that it was actually the fourth day following a severe cold front and marked the first day that the wind had lain down and the sky had clouded up in five days. Information like this is far more pertinent to the fish's activity level

than the simple fact that it was cloudy and seventy-four that day in July you caught all those fish.

FISH THE SINKER. When fishing a worm or jig, don't worry about what a hit feels like. Concentrate on the weight and move it along the bottom by lifting the rod tip from ten o'clock toward eleven o'clock. The higher you lift the weight, the more time it's out of contact with the bottom, and the less feedback about the fish's world it can provide. Keep the movements in the range of a few inches to a foot. Use the weight to feel your way around the bottom, searching for "stuff," and fish it as if you were trying to get snagged. When you run it

across a spot that feels interesting, slow down and be alert. Then cast back to it a few times to feel around even more.

EXPAND YOUR HORIZONS. If you make a point to fish at least a few new waters each year, your knowledge will keep expanding. Keep trying to master more new techniques rather than relying on the ones you're most comfortable with. Bass are flexible and adaptable, as we should be if we hope to catch them.

Weedless topwater plastic frog imitation

EARLY ON, LOOK for the areas that warm the soonest. Dark-bottomed bays, isolated from the main body of water and exposed to the sun, absorb more radiant energy during the day and lose less to the heat-sink effect of the deeper sections of the lake after sundown. Life forms that have wintered in the mud start to rouse as the bottom warms. Soon any fish that are ready to feed are prowling here, and so should you be if you hope to catch them.

When the water warms a bit more, a bass's procreative instincts take over, and the muck-bottomed bays become less appealing than firmer spawning areas. As a nesting fish, the bass must be in water shallow

Easy to Find
Bass are often easiest to find in the spring, when they are predictably nesting in warmer, cleaner areas near some kind of cover.

enough during spawning for sunlight to reach the bottom, and the bottom must be swept clean of silt that would rob the eggs of exposure to the sun. This must be an area where the current is not strong enough to wash eggs out of the nest. And there must be some cover to help protect the nest from creatures that make a springtime living by raiding spawning beds. It's easy to identify these kinds of areas, so finding the fish in spring isn't that difficult.

The question of whether or not to take advantage of fish during the spawn is another matter. In some places, it's legal;

in others, it's not. Biologists tell us that it has little effect on the bass population, because relatively few nests need to be productive to generate enough fry to supply sufficient replacement numbers each year. But some anglers find it distasteful.

Even if you choose not to pursue bass that are actively bedding, as long as bass-fishing season is open, you can target prespawn or postspawn fish because they don't all bed at the same time. Points just outside the spawning areas offer great opportunities to catch bass. Hard and soft jerkbaits are likely choices, as are crankbaits—both diving and lipless varieties—and

topwater plugs. But remember, there are often more bass in a nonaggressive mode than in an aggressive one, so don't forget to give that Texas- or Carolina-rigged worm a shot, too.

As spring wears on, bass need to recuperate from the rigors of spawning, but they also need food. They can be found near whatever source of prey is most abundant and vulnerable. This is why the Slug-Go and other soft jerkbaits were invented. You won't go wrong if you pick one up when the bass start to filter off the beds and don't put it down again until they shift to summer patterns.

A Warm Feeling
The ideal time to fish in spring is on the third sunny day in a row, when the water has warmed. If you can find an area with a black bottom, so much the better.

Spring Fishing

"It was so **still**
I felt like I was sitting
on a sheet of *painted glass.*"

TIME WAS WHEN bass anglers were convinced that the summer's heat sent their quarry into a state of inactivity. Now we know that the opposite is closer to the truth. The bass is a cold-blooded creature, and its metabolism is directly linked to water temperature. The warmer the water (to a point, anyway), the more frequently bass must feed.

Bass move around more in the summer than at any other time of year because of their need to eat. Even though there are differences in the food chain from environment to environment, bass are able to adapt to whatever feeding behavior and

The Food Chain
Learn the fauna of your fishery. If the gizzard shad is abundant, then most bass will respond to crankbait, minnowbait, topwater lures, and plastic minnows.

environmental niche they find advantageous. So it's safe to say that if there's a prey-based pattern, bass are using it during the summer.

Perhaps the most reliable summer patterns revolve around vegetation, because it houses and protects many types of prey, from frogs to panfish to crawfish. Bass prowl the weed beds and their edges, looking for food. Especially when the vegetation forms shade-producing surface mats, it offers hidden vantages for ambush-feeding bass. They position themselves high under

the overhead cover, tight within its most densely shaded area, and then charge out to grab anything swimming by in the lighter open area nearby.

In such areas it's important not to fish beneath the bass, because their feeding focus is rarely downward. They will follow a sinking or diving lure if it passes through their area of surveillance on the way, but if it passes by beneath that window, they will likely not even be aware of it.

Always consider the size of the food-producing area of any shallow cover when searching for summer bass. A bigger weed

bed produces more food than a smaller patch and probably serves as the pantry or dining room for many more fish.

Breaklines and drop-offs are also important elements to consider in summer bass patterns. A breakline is any area where differing habitats meet. A weed edge is the breakline between the vegetated, cover-rich area and the open water next to it. A drop-off is the edge where a shallow, flat bottom falls away into deeper water. A water-color breakline is formed where dingy water meets clear water.

Prey and forage tend to accumulate along the edges of the habitat they prefer, so those edges become prime hunting grounds for predators. Keep in mind that the more severe the difference between the adjoining habitats, the more pronounced the breakline's effect in concentrating prey and bass alike.

Made in the Shade
Bass, especially largemouth, like the shade on a hot summer day. They will hide under it not just to keep cool, but to lie in ambush for a likely meal. One good place to look on any lake would be alongside a grassy or weedy area.

STRATEGIES FOR
Summer Fishing

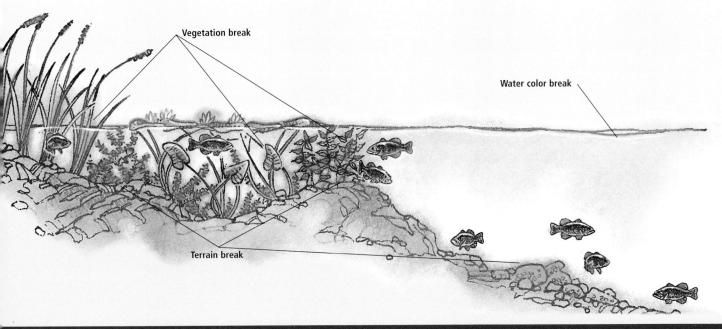

Vegetation break

Water color break

Terrain break

"It was all I could *do* to steer the *beast* away from the shoreline *logs.*"

FOR A BASS, fall officially begins when the water temperature begins to drop more during the night than it warms during the day. Because water is most dense at 39°F, warmer water "floats" on colder water and stays closer to the surface during the summer. That keeps the bottom waters, where decaying organic matter uses oxygen and there's no wave action to replenish it, near the bottom. In many bodies of water, a layer of water with a rapid tempera- ture change forms a barrier that prevents circulation between the warmer water above and the cooler water below. This barrier is called the thermocline.

Once the water temperature trend reverses, however, that surface water begins to sink as it's chilled by the night air. Eventually, the entire layer of water above the thermocline reaches the temperature of the top of the thermocline itself, and continued cooling begins to deteriorate that layer. Wind- driven circulation hastens the

The Moment of Truth
Whether a bass strikes or not often depends on the angler, not the lure. Something is required to trigger a strike. The angler's job is to identify that trigger.

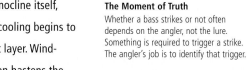
Temperature layers

demise of the thermocline, which eventually ruptures and disintegrates. When this happens, there is nothing to stop the oxygen-deprived, and some- times benzyne-laced, water below from mixing with the water above. If the difference between the two layers is great enough, there can be a sudden drop in water quality. This

STRATEGIES FOR
Fall Fishing

change is stressful for the lake's residents until the autumn winds refresh and mix the water from the top down.

Since there is usually a fishing slump associated with the water turnover, it's best to concentrate on riverine areas. There, current flow prevents thermal stratification in the first place, so the sudden drop in water quality never occurs.

Later in the fall, once the entire water column has been refreshed, bass tend to seek out areas where depth or other factors insulate them from sudden changes in water temperature. Their cold-blooded metabolism doesn't adjust well to sudden changes. Find the areas where conditions are most stable, and you'll usually find groups of bass dense enough to overcome their relative lack of activity in the cold water of late fall. When they are bunched this tightly, the areas they came from are pretty devoid of fish, so most of the lake is a tough row to hoe, fishing-wise. You've got to find the aggregations now, or you'll be fishing where they used to be instead of where they are.

Following the Creek Channel
Reservoir bass often winter at the confluence of a creek channel and the main river channel. Alleyways in the stumps often indicate a creek channel. The depth finder tells the final story.

"We spent our best days *together* in *silence.*"

"Home of crawdads
and *fish* and creatures
from *another world . . .*"

Outboard tach

Outboard hydraulic jack
plate trim control

Engine
temperature
gauge

Speedometer

Liquid crystal sonar

Outboard power
trim gauge

Sonar and global
positioning unit

Sonar tuning
control and
adjustment

Engine water
pressure gauge

Main battery volt gauge

Outboard hydraulic jack
plate trim gauge

Rotating display
"flasher" sonar

Ignition

Fuel gauge

Steering wheel
adjustment control

Master control panel

Hard Copy
Older sonar units (left) are not digital, but
can detect fish just as well and supply a
printout of their readings.

Satellite Technology
All-in-one GPS (Global Positioning System)
units can save hundreds of fishing spots in
their memory.

FISHING WITH
Bells & Whistles

"The moment the *lure*
hit the water near the wing dam,
the *big one* inhaled it."

Flirting with Success

The sky was a cloudless blue and the sun had not yet cleared the hills to the east while I sat waiting for my launch turn in today's tournament. The eerie calls of loons and grebes were interrupted at intervals as, one by one, big bass boats gurgled out of the no-wake zone, then gunned their engines and roared out over the glassy water toward the misty distance. I had little to do but sit and watch, and as I looked around the lake, I noticed two heron along the bank toward the back end of the cove to the left of the launch. Where herons at work are concerned, two are a crowd, and these two were busy eating. I made a mental note.

By the time my launch turn came, I could hardly hide my eagerness. The sun had begun to light the wisps of fog at the far end of the lake. And rather than cranking it up and heading out to open water like all the other boats, I calmly dropped the electric motor and started casting right near the ramp.

Persuaded by those two herons, I would fish my way around the back end of the cove, figuring where there is food, there are bass. That morning I felt like a poker player trying to stay calm while holding a full house. If nothing else, it would keep me out of the heavy boat traffic on the main lake for a while on this warm summer day.

A comfortable casting distance from the bank where the herons had been working, the water was about five feet deep. There was some submerged weed growth and scattered brush half in the water at the shoreline. A solitary frog croaked urgently near a large fallen tree that lay half in the water and had long since begun to rot. This seemed like the perfect location to try to entice enough scrappy bass to fill the well. And if luck was with me, that's exactly what would happen.

Willow Leaf Spinnerbait with Trailer

PRO TIPS

In the fall, keep an eye out for flocks of feeding gulls. Often, a school of surface-feeding bass is just below, forcing fleeing baitfish to the surface.

SATISFACTION

To many, fishing is an experience to be shared with friends and family, and as much satisfaction can come from a well-placed cast as from landing a lunker.

I had already rigged my rods with a number of lures, and I grabbed one with a bright, flashy spinnerbait. Just a few casts into the morning, a fish rolled off a submerged stick to take a halfhearted swipe at my plug and missed. It set my heart racing, but more work around the stick produced no response, and the frog had gone quiet. *Okay. Let's try another rig*, I told myself. So I picked up a rod rigged with a natural-colored soft jerkbait, hoping an image more vulnerable than the spinning blades might be attractive. I brought the lure by the cover and let it break, die, and sink out of sight for a few seconds. Then I gently twitched it. Still no takers. A bit farther along the bank, I traded my tandem-bladed bait for one with a single blade and a more subdued hue. Since my earlier volunteer had

responded to a kind of natural-looking lure, I was hopeful. But after two empty casts, then three more, I decided to take advantage of a single-bladed lure's better action on the sink and switched my retrieve technique to one with more pauses and twitches in it. I kept my fingers crossed that this would change my luck. At the rate I was going it would take all day to fill the well, if I could fill it at all.

As I worked the lure along the bank, my thoughts began to take on a rhythm all their own. This bank reminded me of one my partner and I had fished years before during a smaller tournament. In that event, I was a "back-deck angler." I found myself smiling with the memory of that day's activity: "There's one!" my partner had hollered. "I think that's a bite." Extending his rod tip toward the shoreline, he braced his feet, leaned way over in its

Weedless Plastic Worm

P R O   T I P S

You're a disturbance to the scene, so master equipment meant for a long-distance cast. You'll surprise and catch more fish.

SOLITUDE

When you want your solitude broken by the company of a bass, fish the reeds with a weedless plastic worm (above) or work a topwater spoon or imitation frog among the water lotus (facing page).

direction, and waited. "Yeah, that's a fish." Slowly he began reeling in slack, then he paused. "Nah, maybe it's just the grass. No, it's moving. Yeah, look at my line go!" he chortled, as he gingerly raised his rod tip, only to drop it again as soon as he thought he felt resistance. "I think he dropped it. No, there he is, he's still got it." This little conversation with himself went on a full minute. In that time, I had finished my cast, inched across the bottom, and made another.

My partner was still waiting to decide where he really had that fish, when I felt a slight thump on my jig. I reared back with an instant hookset. It wasn't a huge fish, so I tried to hurry it to the boat to keep it out of the way of whatever my partner was doing. I had it about two-thirds of the way in when I heard my partner say, "There he

goes. He's really got it now!" That's when he set the hook—into the mouth of the very fish I was just about to reach down and lip land. We had quite a discussion in the boat over who had caught that fish.

I still insist that if I hadn't jerked on it so hard, he'd still be wondering if it was time to set the hook. Remembering that day makes me laugh out loud. We were both lucky, really. Lucky to have caught that fish at all and lucky for the memory. It's been fifteen years since that tournament, and he still insists he caught that fish.

Most of the time luck isn't that evenly distributed. I once won a two-day team tournament in which my partner caught only five fish during the competition while I caught and culled through more than thirty. We were both fishing the same lures, and we were saturating the same little corner of a cove with casts, repeatedly fishing the same water. So it wasn't a matter

of me getting to new water before he did. It was just Lady Luck. And that day, she was all mine.

But luck is a fickle lady. Some years later, in a team tournament on the Hudson River in the late fall, I was fishing with another partner. He and I usually relied on light tackle and small grubs in the fall on the Hudson, and we did very well with it. We had pulled into Esopus Creek after breaking off two fish in the first hour and boating none. My partner decided to switch to a heavy rod with 20-pound test line and a half-ounce jig and pig. "I might not get bit again today," he said, "but if I do, I know it's coming into the boat." Though fishing wasn't fast that day, he caught nine bass on that jig and pig over the next six and a half hours. When it got to be four fish to none and, hoping to turn luck my way, I switched from my little grub to a duplicate of what he was using. Two hours later, and now down eight to nothing, I switched back and finally caught one little twelve-inch bass. The ten fish we weighed in went thirty-five pounds, and though we easily won the tournament, my contribution had weighed less than a pound. We had fished the same spots and, for most of the day, used the same technique. But as luck would have it, the fish were having none of me that day, although they sure did like most of what my partner was doing.

My reverie was suddenly cut short by a hit on my line. Was this another volunteer? No, just a snag. Clearly, Lady Luck was out flirting with some other fisherman. The only thing filling my well today would be memories—but that's okay, too!

—*Rich Zaleski*

Trimming the jig skirt a quarter inch below the bend in the hook gives it a pulsating action as it swims through the water.

IMAGINATION

When you create a mental picture of cover as it extends underwater, you can better position your first cast to trigger that elusive lunker.

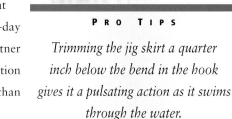

Reels
Modern reels (left and below left) are marvels of strength, speed, and efficiency.

Fishing Line
Today's lines range from super-strong steel fibers to invisible-as-glass clear monofilament.

READY FOR ANY SITUATION
An avid angler's tackle room may include an array of combinations as diverse as they are personal.

RIGGED AND READY
Amateur anglers are increasingly following the lead of the pros. The average bass boat deck (facing page) holds combinations of rods, reels, and line for any fishing condition.

TOOLS OF THE TRADE
Rods & Reels

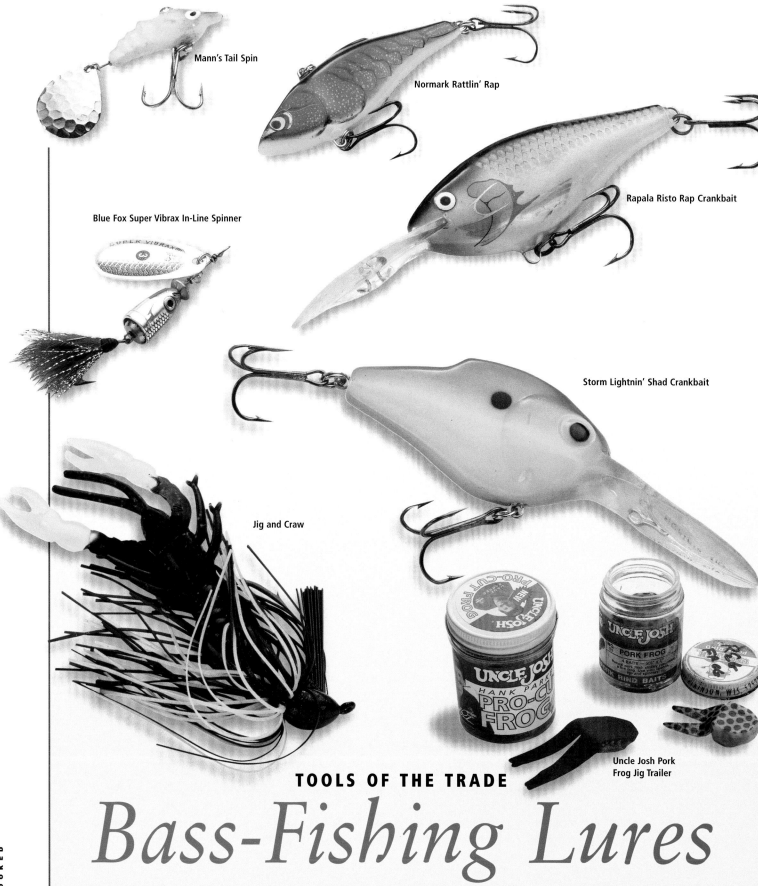

Mann's Tail Spin

Normark Rattlin' Rap

Rapala Risto Rap Crankbait

Blue Fox Super Vibrax In-Line Spinner

Storm Lightnin' Shad Crankbait

Jig and Craw

Uncle Josh Pork Frog Jig Trailer

TOOLS OF THE TRADE

Bass-Fishing Lures

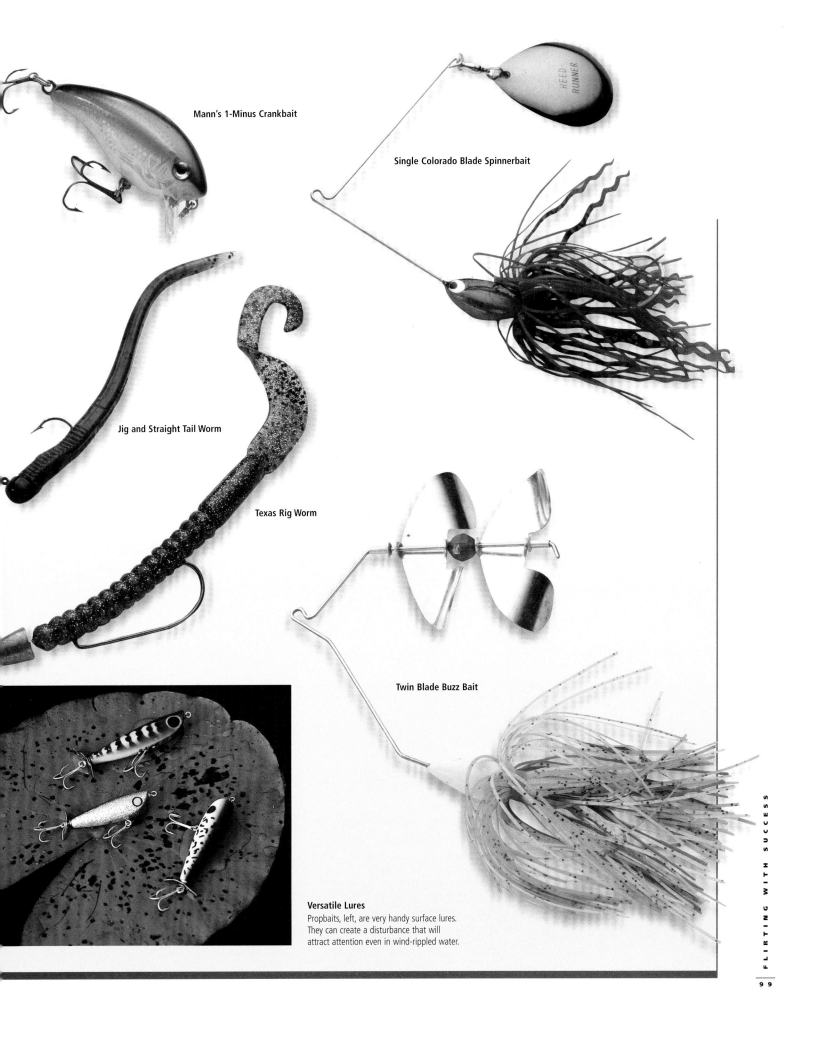

Mann's 1-Minus Crankbait

Single Colorado Blade Spinnerbait

Jig and Straight Tail Worm

Texas Rig Worm

Twin Blade Buzz Bait

Versatile Lures
Propbaits, left, are very handy surface lures.
They can create a disturbance that will
attract attention even in wind-rippled water.

" I watched her *rise*
to the lure
and study it."

BASS FISHING REQUIRES a variety of casting skills because of the diversity of habitats in which the fish live and their ever-changing disposition and activity level. There are five basic casts most used in bass fishing. The most common is the two-handed overhead cast. Then come the pitch, flip, skip, and roll casts.

When bass are actively feeding—that is, when they're flushing and chasing forage species in open, relatively clear, deep water—long casts are more important than accurate ones. But when inactive bass are suspended beside shallow cover, accuracy is critical to reaching in their shrunken strike zone.

Speed and Skill
Backlash control is very important with baitcaster spools that can turn up to twenty thousand rpm.

The two-handed overhead cast is relatively inaccurate, but it gets the most distance. When extra-long casts are necessary, experienced anglers normally use 6½- to 7-foot, medium-action rods with long handles.

But when bass are relating to shallow cover and a quiet, accurate presentation is critical, it's best to rely on the pitch and flip casts. With both techniques, you use the rod tip to create a pendulum action, which sends the lure along a low trajectory toward the target. Although

flipping allows you to cover shallow, nearby targets more quickly than pitching, it's limited to off-color water. When targeting heavy cover in relatively clear water, pitching is more appropriate because it allows you to cast from farther out. With both techniques, use heavy-action rods, baitcast reels with low gear ratios, and strong, abrasion-resistant fishing lines.

Skip and roll casts are also useful when working in, around, and under cover. With this technique, shorter rods (6 to

6$\frac{1}{2}$ feet) with shorter handles are best because they are more maneuverable. With a quick, underhanded roll of the wrist, you can skip or "flick" a lure a good distance back under a low, overhanging obstruction. Spin and spincast outfits with revolving spools (baitcast reels tend to overrun and backlash) will accurately and quietly place lures in the tightest pockets of cover.

For the best accuracy, distance, and presentation from each cast, the rod, reel, and fishing line must match the job. You also want to be able to switch tactics in a hurry. This is a good reason to carry a number of rods, each equipped with an appropriate reel and line for the various casts you may want to try. ✦

Smallmouth Specialties
Spinning, baitcast, and fly tackle (below) are all well suited for smallmouth, which respond to smaller lures.

MAKING THE PITCH
Casting Techniques

Pitching to a Pocket
Pitching is a very effective way to penetrate heavy cover by targeting the small holes and pockets other methods can't reach.

"Sometimes you find **bass.** Always, you find **yourself.**"

FLY-FISHING FOR trout is steeped in its own style and rituals, but bass anglers tend to care less about style and more about having fun. Of course, there's more than simply a difference in attitude separating these two forms of fly-fishing. There are differences in approach and equipment. Unlike the whiplike rods, dainty tippets, and tiny flies associated with trout, fly-fishing for bass is typified by heavy rods, full-sinking lines, and bulky, wind-resistant flies.

Admittedly, an 8-weight fly line awkwardly delivering a water-logged, rabbit-fur leech to a grass edge is somewhat lacking in the rhythms and beauty normally associated with fly-fishing for trout. When fly-fishing for bass, function—not art—is what counts. The heavier equipment, cover-filled habitat, and headstrong disposition of the fish make fly-fishing for bass a very physical game. Fortunately, modern graphite rods and high-tech fly lines make casting large bass easier than in the past. Still, a moderate-size largemouth can quickly humble the most confident fly angler outfitted in the best equipment.

Although most fly anglers rarely fish deeper than the first foot or two from the water's surface, some of the better bass are taken on flies

Waiting in the Weeds
Big bass in shallow water and a snag-free floating fly line are a fly fisherman's recipe for a memorable match.

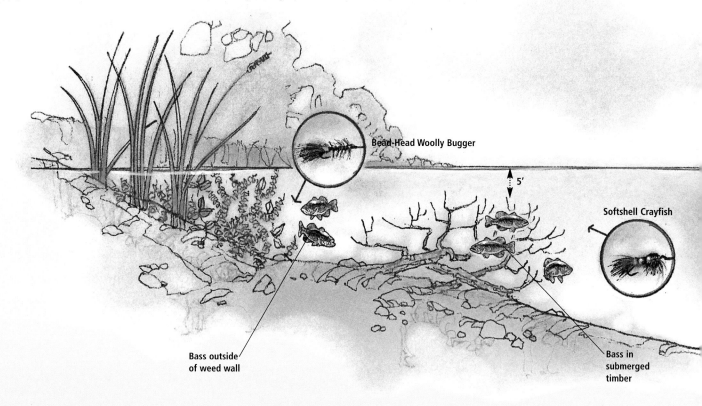

Bead-Head Woolly Bugger

5'

Softshell Crayfish

Bass outside of weed wall

Bass in submerged timber

ON THE FLY
Fly-Fishing Techniques

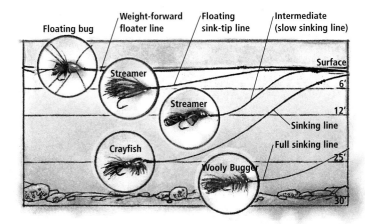

Floating bug · **Weight-forward floater line** · **Floating sink-tip line** · **Intermediate (slow sinking line)**

Streamer

Surface

Streamer

6'

12'

Sinking line

Crayfish

Full sinking line

Wooly Bugger

25'

30'

fished four to twelve feet deep. Modern full-sinking fly lines not only sink faster, they do so in a way that allows anglers to place their flies as much as twenty-five feet deep.

Popular bass flies accurately mimic the action and appearance of many conventional lures. There are fly patterns that closely imitate the plastic worm, spinnerbait, jig and pig, and

jerkbait. And flies are more life-like than plastic lures. When bass are actively feeding, move-ment seems more important than appearance. But when bass are inactive, a lifelike fly often scores more strikes.

Fly anglers are also better able to control the depth of the presentation. Most of the time, this is determined by the sink rate of the fly line. By fishing a neutrally buoyant fly with a sinking tip or an inter-mediate sinking fly line, or a weighted fly behind a floating

line, you can suspend the fly in the water column. When bass are inactive, this ability to suspend the lure in the strike zone can give you an edge.

Of course, the greatest reason to pick up a fly rod is the opportunity for an intimate battle with the fish. Beginning with the hookset and finishing with the close-quarters battle, you have your hand on the pulse of the bass itself. The challenge of landing a real lunker from cover on a fly rod is an experience all bass anglers should know.

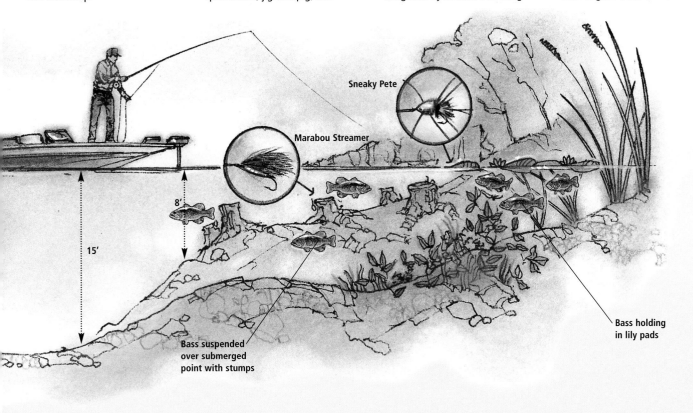

Sneaky Pete

Marabou Streamer

8'

15'

Bass suspended over submerged point with stumps

Bass holding in lily pads

Bass Slider

Puglasi Baitfish

Crystal Rabbit

Bass Slider

Wool Shad

Flash Bang

Nix's Sunfish

Weedless Rabbit Bugger

Weedless Rabbit Bugger

Weedless Frog

Deerhair Frog

Cigar Box of Memories
Antique flies like these, which sit in their box like a treasured insect collection, are collectors' items. Skillfully tied by patient hands, these flies were catching bass half a century ago.

TOOLS OF THE TRADE
Fly-Fishing Lures

Foam Pike Diver

Big Fish Foam Popper

Pete's Slider

Dalberg Rabbit Diver

Swimming Baitfish

Big Fish Diver

Pearly Popper

Deer Hair Popper

33 Special

Hard Foam Popper

Softex Popper

Foam Chugger

Deer Hair Popper

Whit's Hair Bug

Rabbit Crayfish

Tan Zonker

Olive Zonker

Brown Chernobyl Hair Head

Chernobyl Hair Head

Fly Reel Placement
The fly reel sits below the handgrip to balance the longer fly rod. A fly-fishing reel does little but hold line. When casting, anglers pull the length of line that they plan to cast off the reel by hand because, unlike a conventional bass lure, a fly is too light to pull line off the reel.

period on either side of the day of a full or new moon. In fact, the long-standing 1932 world-record largemouth came just two days before a full moon.

Choose a device or table that limits its scope to the moon's phases and its rising and setting. It should not include the added effects of computer models or

CONSIDER THIS: when the moon is directly overhead, the ground beneath our feet is raised as much as a foot. If lunar gravity can influence the solid ground that much, just think what effect it must have on water and on the fish that live there.

Many anglers believe that most fish-spawning activity is somehow keyed to the full or dark moon. Records confirm these times as the periods of strongest tides as well as of volcanic eruptions and earthquakes. When compared with complete lunar data, the International Game Fish Association's world records set over a ten-year period indicate that 73 percent of these fish were caught within a three-day

traditional preconceptions regarding dawn and dusk, seasons, or the influence of the sun.

Each month, consider the three days on either side of the days of the full and new moons to be the best, with a special emphasis on the three days leading up to the full moon and the three days after the new moon.

Plan your vacations and expensive trips with these times of the month in mind. This is the time to emphasize larger, more realistic lures fished at a slower, more seductive pace, and it is the best time of all to fish live bait. Soft plastics are a great choice, but trolling large minnow-type lures like six- to seven-inch A. C. Shiners or Rapalas can be effective, too. This is the time of the month when the best daily (moon-up/moon-down) periods occur around noon, and the good visibility makes a realistic, or live-bait, approach your best chance for big bass.

Generally, on all other fishing days, remain conscious of when the moon is either straight up or straight down. The daily activity periods last an average of two hours each, so slow down and go to the plastic worm, jig, tube lure, soft jerkbait, or any of the other more realistic, finesse presentations.

Irresistible
Large live minnows are an ideal bait for lunkers during the active lunar cycles.

LUNAR INFLUENCES

Minding the Moon

"*A solitary frog was croaking urgently...*"

"*I think we both knew* ***then*** *that we'd never forget that* **moment.**"

Time
on the
Water

My nose ached sharply with each breath as the frigid wind swept away the smell of the steel gray water. I stood alone on the open deck of my bass boat, three thousand feet above sea level in the lonely gloom just before dawn. Rolling out of my warm bed at three o'clock, I'd driven more than an hour to launch my boat off the sloppy wet launch ramp and spend the next twelve hours relentlessly casting an eight-inch imitation trout that swam better than those with a heartbeat. With each cast I strove for precision in its placement, entry, and retrieval. Constantly adjusting my position to maintain the best stance, I was ready to drive home the 4/0 treble hook the instant the strike came. Huge bass are often caught in miserable weather, and by that standard, today was promising. It was the dark of the moon, too. Another positive sign. I was happy.

Empty-handed, I left the lake at sundown, my forehead furrowed with tension and my right

shoulder aching. I had never gotten bit, had never even seen a fish; but it was a good day nonetheless because I had paid another installment on the dues required to eventually catch a giant bass.

Largemouth bass fishing requires paying your dues. It also requires the ability to think, and although a few professionals seem instinctively to make good decisions, no one beats the bass all the time. And no one can guarantee success. If catching fish is the measure, then most of us lose the game more than we win. But the catch isn't all there is. Sometimes it's the encounter with the wilderness that's the prize.

A few weeks after that lonely, cold day, my teenage daughter, Amy, and I found ourselves fishing in a warm midmorning drizzle. Spring had taken over with zeal like a genie let loose after being bottled up a thousand years too long. The shore along the bank was alive with green grass and yellow buds. Earth seemed to be stretching languidly, as if awakening from a nap.

From the side of the boat, I watched Amy's minnow bait hit the water within the ring of a raindrop. It floated until its own water rings dissipated. And for a few moments, the only sound we heard was the rain. Then Amy made the bait twitch once, and there was an explosion of water and bass that shattered the stillness. For an electrifying moment, a two-pound fish danced on its tail, then dove and set out to drag the offending bait down to the muddy lake bottom. But in the shallow water there was little room for a sustained fight, and within a few minutes I was gently releasing the feisty green male from my daughter's line.

P R O   T I P S

The runoff caused by a storm can stimulate the bass's bite. Anytime there is an influx of water coming into a major creek or smaller cut or wash, the bass will run to it.

FISHING ACCESSORIES

Useful fishing tools for any day on the water include nail clippers for line, stainless steel longnose pliers, a portable scale, hemostats, and a hook sharpener.

As was our custom, Amy thanked the fish for the meeting, and then we happily sent it back to tell its hidden brothers a harrowing tale of alien abduction.

Over the next few hours, we repeated this ritual again and again: quiet casts followed by a subtle movement of the floating plug and attacks by junkyard dogs that looked like bass. But these bass weren't hungry. They had finished their winter gorging on crawdads and deep schools of bait and had then resettled to the shallows to nest. These were territorial strikes.

The sound of a raven screaming on the nearby shore caused us to look away from our pursuit. It was on top of a small hill, caught in an ugly tangle of old fishing line. The big black bird was leaping frantically into the air in awkward pitches, then falling back to the ground. It was clear from its struggle and cries that it was tiring and would soon die without help.

Amy and I quickly beached the boat and started to climb the small hill spiked with twisted manzanita brush to reach the struggling bird. Our approach only heightened the raven's distress, and we were afraid it would hurt itself more. Up close, the bird was much larger than I had expected, almost the size of a small dog. Its coal black eyes alternately fixed on each of us, as if trying to decide which one it would take out first. I asked Amy to go back to the boat, but she refused and we had no time to argue.

The bird we now faced was no longer a victim. It snapped savagely with its sharp beak, ready to tear at anything it could reach. Three hearts were now racing. Amy and I whispered our strategy. She waved her hands and screamed, and when the bird

responded, I reached toward it with my landing net. The raven turned and attacked the net, tearing a section as easily as if it were a cobweb. This was a scene out of a nightmare. Suddenly the big bird went still. The silence made us wonder if it had died.

I carefully inspected the raven to see if it was really dead, when one of its black eyes took a bead on me and its panting body, mustering its last bit of strength, attacked. Amy and I responded by holding the bird down with what was left of the frayed net. Amy kept pressure on the raven as I quickly cut the tangled line from its legs. Putting my daughter behind me, I lifted the net and the bird lunged to our right, taking off with a final scream.

We watched until it disappeared over the trees. Then, in silence, we walked back down the hill to the boat. Today, neither of us can remember if we made any more casts that day. And since then, Amy and I have gone fishing countless times and we've collected many more stories to tell. But in sharing them with friends or repeating them to each other, our most prized is the catch and release of the raven.

—*Kevin Mineo*

PRO TIPS

When water temperature drops, fish feed slower. Make your bait cover the same distance in more time.

LASTING MEMORIES

Fishing can create bonds that last for a lifetime and often proves that the thrill of the catch brings the same glee to all, regardless of the age of the angler.

"We were *wet,*
hungry, thirsty, tired,
sore, and
deliriously *happy.*"

SUPERSTITION AND luck are pretty much different sides of the same coin. Athletes, gamblers, and anglers all have a good share of superstition, which is really just a kind of ritual to attract luck. And why not? Often, it seems as if you can do everything just right and still not succeed. Besides, so many things are beyond our control, like the weather and the fact that you can't buy a bite when the livewell of the boat twenty feet away is brimming with bass and they're using the same lures you are. It's no wonder anglers have so many tricks—and as many rituals—to try to get the fish gods on our side.

For example, bananas are thought to bring bad luck. Captains on sport boats have been known to look through every passenger's lunch and

Fisherman's Choice
Many fishermen might not admit it, but just any hat won't do for a day on the water. It has to be a lucky hat.

throw the offending fruit overboard. Some pros have even hidden bananas on competitors' boats before a tournament.

Wetting a net before you need to use it is supposed to bring good luck. So is spitting on a lure. But taking a camera along is bad luck—kind of like counting your chips before the card game's done.

Many people consider catching a fish on the first cast of the day bad luck. So these folks make the first cast short and to deep water and then reel it back as quickly as possible. You can fish against the wind, but don't whistle in that direction, or luck will leave. And don't even bother going to the lake if the cows are lying down. This

last one may well be fact, since major feeding periods for many creatures are affected by lunar phases, and fishermen figure if the cows aren't eating, the fish probably aren't either.

Some fishermen have favorite clothes or hats, and sometimes you can recognize them a mile away, since they're afraid to wash out the good luck. Others will only release fish later, in another part of the lake, believing that the fish talk to one another. Some anglers must fish out of a clean boat, their gear must be neat and orderly, their clothing sharp and fresh. But don't pet the dog or you won't catch a single fish.

Good luck or bad luck can also be created. If we think our lucky hat will get us bites, we may fish with more confidence and catch more fish. The opposite could also be true. Our attitude affects our performance in everything we do. Or perhaps it's simply just as the wise old fisherman says, "The harder you work, the luckier you get."

Keeping Luck in Your Grasp
Releasing a fish on the same side of the boat as it was caught is a must for some superstitious anglers.

FINGERS CROSSED

Fishermen's Luck

ABSOLUTES DON'T EXIST, including a "perfect" lunch, but some combinations come close. Because successful bass fishing requires constant mental and physical attention, sitting on a bank waiting for the little bell at the end of your rod to ring is rarely part of this sport.

During tournaments, eating and drinking are secondary until the boats are gathered and you're waiting to be pulled out of the water. The intensity of competition can be so high that fishermen at weigh-ins often find themselves parched and suddenly realize they haven't taken a drink all day. But, then, there are moments during the heat of tournament battle when you can manage a swig of an electrolyte-rich power drink or maybe even some homemade lemonade to help wash down a granola bar, candy bar, or a small sandwich.

A day on the lake bass fishing with the family, or on those nontournament outings, can bring some of the sweetest rewards. One of them is a lunch packed to the gills with hoagies stuffed with ham and cheese, beef, or pastrami; sandwiches made on fresh French bread or sourdough stuffed with tangy deviled egg or meatball, sausage, and peppers; or— always a favorite—peanut butter and fresh apple. Of course, these staples can be accompanied by fruit pies and peanut butter cookies. A picnic in the boat or on the bank makes for one delightful day.

Feeding Body and Soul
Enjoying the outdoors doesn't mean going without conveniences, but, of course, it does involve leaving it litter-free.

THE PERFECT
Fishing Lunch

Comforts of Home
Ingenuity and improvisation can make lunch
a special occasion on a wilderness trip.

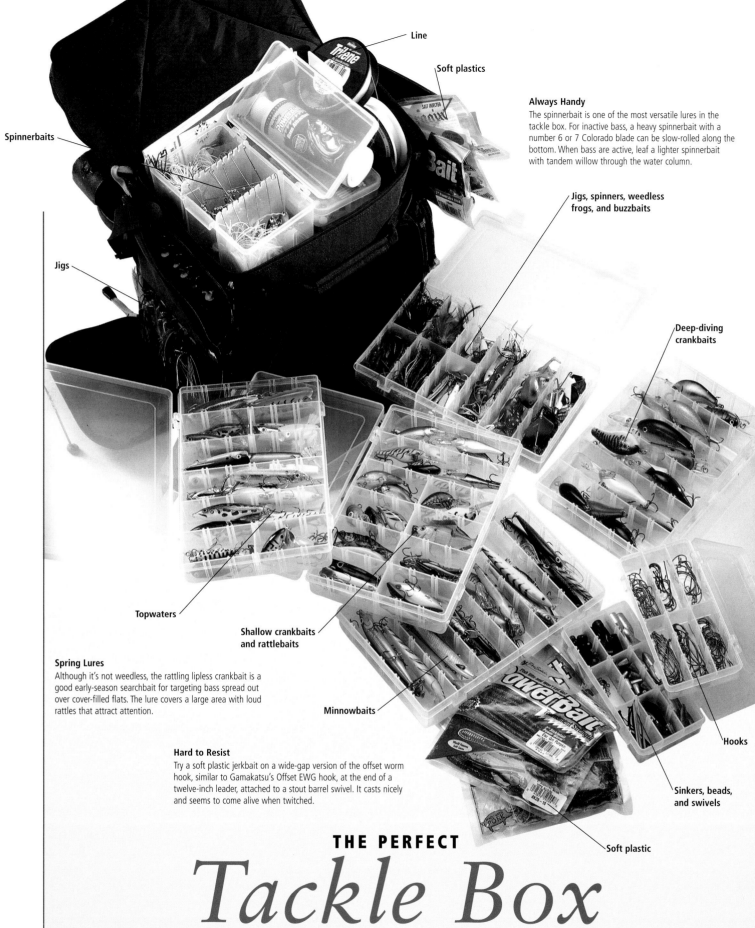

Line

Soft plastics

Spinnerbaits

Always Handy
The spinnerbait is one of the most versatile lures in the tackle box. For inactive bass, a heavy spinnerbait with a number 6 or 7 Colorado blade can be slow-rolled along the bottom. When bass are active, leaf a lighter spinnerbait with tandem willow through the water column.

Jigs, spinners, weedless frogs, and buzzbaits

Jigs

Deep-diving crankbaits

Topwaters

Shallow crankbaits and rattlebaits

Spring Lures
Although it's not weedless, the rattling lipless crankbait is a good early-season searchbait for targeting bass spread out over cover-filled flats. The lure covers a large area with loud rattles that attract attention.

Minnowbaits

Hooks

Hard to Resist
Try a soft plastic jerkbait on a wide-gap version of the offset worm hook, similar to Gamakatsu's Offset EWG hook, at the end of a twelve-inch leader, attached to a stout barrel swivel. It casts nicely and seems to come alive when twitched.

Sinkers, beads, and swivels

Soft plastic

THE PERFECT
Tackle Box

TIME ON THE WATER

"The **biggest** one hit hard on my last **cast** of the day."

REMEMBER THE LAST time you got caught out on the lake in the rain? Starting out, it looked like such a nice day, and although you hadn't checked the weather beforehand, what could happen? You saw a few clouds headed off to the northwest, and a few more higher up that were on their way straight north, but the sun was shining through. On your way to the lake that morning, you probably didn't stop to notice the static on the AM radio. And you certainly didn't pay much attention to the way the smoke from that coal-fired power plant was hovering around the same height as the smokestack as it drifted toward the west. The signs of bad weather were all there, but you didn't see them. So how can you know once you're out on a lake or river if you're likely to be chased off the water in a few hours by a thunderstorm? It's simple: watch the sky.

Weather change occurs from the top of the atmosphere down, and wind change portends weather change. When you see several layers of clouds in the sky moving in different directions, pay attention. You can see the wind change coming in those clouds. If the wind shifts in a counterclockwise direction in the Northern Hemisphere, bad weather *is* coming. If you look at the shore and see the leaves on the trees, which tend to grow according to prevailing winds, turning their backs in a gust, the weather is liable to deteriorate.

Other signs include the buildup of towering, darkening cumulus clouds, or clouds moving from the east or northeast, or a halo around the moon. Look into the distance. Do faraway objects seem to stand above the horizon? Can you suddenly hear distant sounds very clearly? These signs could mean rain, just as wind from the south with clouds moving from the west, a yellow sunset, or clouds with sharp, clearly defined edges are often indicators of high winds in the offing.

But look at the bright side. When smoke and cloud bases rise and the southerly wind shifts to the west, nature is forecasting clearing weather. And a red sky to the east and clear to the west at sunset means it is likely to stay that way.

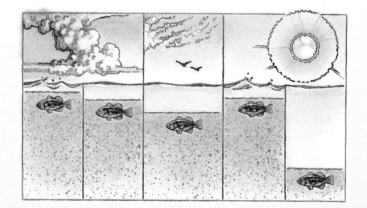

Reading the Signs

Wind from the north, don't venture forth.
Wind from the east, fish bite least.
Wind from the south blows the bait in the fish's mouth.
Wind from the west, fish bite the best.

Wind Wisdom
Look for shifting winds. Wind rotates around storms, so if wind direction stays constant for a long period of time near a disturbance, it could mean the bad weather is headed right at you.

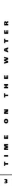

THE UNIQUE SOUTHWEST experience of fishing for trophy bass at night began in the early 1990s. Whether measured by numbers or size, the results were phenomenal. Typically, the most productive lakes for giant bass are clear and tend to stock trout, as if they were a sport fish that someone wanted to catch. Bass want to catch these trout and in the process they grow into strong young fish that exceed ten pounds, with small heads and football bodies.

Tactics are simple but effective. Black lights mounted on both sides of the bow and stern transform the line into green rope against black water and make for easy observation. The best bait is an eight-inch black worm Texas-rigged on 15-pound fluorescent line. Jigs trailed

with black pork, big slow-rolled spinnerbaits, and cranks can also produce, but the worm generally outperforms all else. Like the first Ford Model-T, you can use any color as long as it's black. Your contrast is the moon and the sky.

With the black light, every contact, including a pickup by a bass, sends a visual signal that broadcasts thirty feet away. It's important to see the bite before

both you and the fish feel it. Bass have to be given more time after dark to eat the bait. If they feel any tension, they will often spit the worm before you can react. If you give yourself the opportunity to set the hook after the fish has held the bait a little longer, the fish is often swimming away as the hook seeks purchase. This means there's a better chance of a

hookup than if the fish is coming toward you and just picking up the bait.

It may be hard to do, but forget the daytime fishing pattern. Bass move up at night to feed, and that stump in twenty feet of water will be abandoned. Shallow rocks hold the day's heat a little longer. Crawdads forage there at night, and bass will follow. A nice drop-off nearby is a bonus, and a transition zone between a stretch of riprap or a dam and a steep bank can make your trip.

Small fish tactics won't work here. Hooks should be stout 3/0 to 5/0. You must drive the point into the more substantial jaw of a fish over eight pounds. When you set the hook, tell yourself you're fishing for the heads.

Here are the keys for big Southwestern bass at night: Fish the nights from two days before a full moon to two days after, fish a clear lake, use black worms on stout hooks, see the bite with black lights and fluorescent line, and bring a strong heart.

Slow and Easy
Slow-moving lures that give bass plenty of time to find them and are easy to catch are the best way to hook a lunker at night.

LUNKERS BY MOONLIGHT
Fishing at Night

MARRY THE BANK. If you always cast to the bank, most of the time there will be more fish behind you than in front of you. There are as many edges and targets to cast to away from the bank; they just require a little more effort to bump your lure into. The fish living at those spots aren't beaten over the head with lures every weekend like the ones tucked up against the shoreline, and may be less educated and easier to catch.

AVOID THE BANK. Ignoring the fish that live along the shoreline is just as bad as ignoring the ones that don't. Bass love breaklines, and the shoreline is the ultimate breakline, so there are almost always some there. They are the easiest ones to find and get fished the hardest, but they can also give you a quick feel for the activity and position of the fish that day.

PLAY TUG-OF-WAR. When you think you have a bite, there's nothing to be gained by waiting for a fish to give you confirming evidence. A fish will often swim around with a lure in its mouth for quite a while (yes, even without the benefit of chemical enhancements like scent and taste additives) and pull your rod tip down as it swims. And sometimes the bass will just spit the lure out at the first sign that something's not right. The instant you think you have a bite, set the hook.

ACCEPT CONVENTIONAL WISDOM AT FACE VALUE. Many things that most anglers take as gospel are questionable, and some are patently false. Too often, such statements are self-fulfilling prophecies.

BELIEVE THAT FISH THINK AS WE DO. Fish don't think. They simply react to conditions and events that affect them. Their reactions are controlled by the behavior model formed by their instincts, basic nature, and acquired traits. Ascribing human traits to fish leads you away from consistent success rather than toward it.

LEAVE BITING FISH. Unless you're practicing for a tournament and

need to expand a pattern in a hurry, catch the ones you've found first, before you try to duplicate the conditions elsewhere.

FORCE YOUR PRECONCEPTIONS ON THE FISH. Advance planning is great. But deciding ahead of time where the fish will be and how you'll catch them is foolhardy. Fish according to what the fish want, not according to what you had envisioned.

CAST TO MEMORIES. Last year was last year, and the spots that were good then might not be all that great this year. There aren't any secrets on the water. The hotter a spot or pattern, the more likely that a lot more anglers than you and your buddies were out there taking advantage of it. Give it a shot, but if it doesn't pan out quickly, be prepared to move on to Plan B.

OVERLOOK INCOMING WATER. Never pass by a flowing stream mouth, gurgling spring, drainage ditch, or even an industrial discharge without stopping to put a lure into or near it a couple

BAD HABITS

Catch Fewer Fish

of times. If the water is noticeably warmer, cooler, clearer, or muddier—so much the better.

IGNORE THE LAKE'S OTHER RESIDENTS. Too many bass anglers ignore the lake's other species in their single-minded pursuit of bass. Time spent pursuing bluegill, crappie, perch, striper, pike, or whatever else is swimming around in that environment helps you better understand the aquatic web and, indirectly, gives you more insight into the behavior patterns of the bass who live there as well. And it's a lot of fun, too.

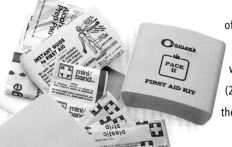

THE MOST IMPORTANT ingredient for a good day on the water is safety. All life may have emerged from the water, but it is no longer our natural element, and a good day on the lake can turn bad in the blink of an eye if you're not prepared. Preparation and common sense are your best allies. Common sense is up to you, but here are a few safety tips to help you prepare for the usual hazards and for some things that might come up unexpectedly. These tips won't help you catch bigger bass, but they will make you a better angler.

INSTALL HANDLES. If the passenger seats in the boat don't have handles nearby for rough-water situations, install them.

CARRY ANCHORS AND ROPES. In case the engine dies in rough water, always have an anchor of adequate weight to hold the boat, with enough rope (200 feet) to keep the bow riding high.

GET A MARINE-BAND RADIO. Nothing brings help faster than Channel 16, the emergency band. Coast Guard stations, local charters, and authorities monitor this band. In heavy fog on big water, it lets nearby ships know you're there.

USE A SPOTLIGHT. Spotlights can be lifesavers in the dark. Get a powerful beam (500,000 to 1 million candlepower) that plugs into the outlet for your trolling motor. You want to see shore and rocks and logs before you hit them!

USE SUNSCREEN. Select one with a high SPF rating unless you plan to fish from under a bridge all day—and especially if you're going to be on the water for longer than a day. Take off your shirt and apply the lotion before you leave your home or hotel. Don't forget your nose and the tops of your ears.

PROTECT YOUR EYES. Wear good ski goggles whenever the boat is moving. They are relatively inexpensive, and some are even made to fit over sunglasses.

HIDE YOUR HOOKS. There's nothing like a recently sharpened treble hook sticking out of your thumb to get your attention. Hang lures tied to rods on the underside of the reel against the butt when you're not using them. Specially made Velcro pouches are good for this purpose, and even a piece of tinfoil can give some protection.

SECURE EVERYTHING IN THE BOAT. Most modern bass boats have straps built in for rods, but everything else, including tackle, should be tied down while the boat is moving. If anything can fall out if the boat turns upside down, you're not there yet.

TREAT YOUR WOUNDS WHEN THE DAY IS DONE. Treat small cuts fishing has wrought—especially any caused by a bass. Wrap them up at night and again in the morning. You'll be more comfortable and fish better.

KNOW WHAT TO DO WHEN YOU'RE SWAMPED. When a wave goes over the boat, keep going! Keep the engine revved up, and transfer all passengers and deck weight possible to the bow. Try to get the boat level, and turn on the bilge pumps. Get the boat into shallower water out of the wind as soon as possible and continue to circle until the pump (and some bailing) clears the water from the decks.

RECORD WAYPOINTS. GPS is also a safety feature. Besides recording routes through treacherous waters, it gets you back to the dock. Always punch in a waypoint at the landing, even on familiar water. Things look different in darkness and in fog.

ALWAYS WEAR LIFE VESTS UNDER POWER. Other boaters, dangerous waves, driver error, drivers showing off—any number of things can put you in the drink.

Lifeline
High-performance boats will continue to run in tight circles, making it impossible for an overboard operator to escape. Always wear a life lanyard hooked to a kill switch.

FISHING REMINDERS
Safety Tips

"We came home **smiling.**
Our creel was empty,
but our hearts were *full.*"

ONE FRIDAY AFTERNOON after a hard day's work, I decided I had earned a little break to go fishing the next day. My wife agreed to the terms (I promised to be home early to get some chores done around the house) and woke me that morning at three. She made a small snack and packed some water in my lunch kit. Thirty minutes later I grabbed my truck and boat keys, kissed her good-bye, and went out to unhook the battery charger. While doing so, I observed the boat leaning precariously to the right. Further inspection revealed a nearly flat tire on that side. No problem; I pulled out the old pump and in ten minutes was on my way.

The smell of the morning air as I headed to the lake did not alert me to the coming surprises, or I would have turned around and gone home. The only decent ramp on the lake had increased the launch fee by two dollars, so I wrote a lengthy explanation on a piece of paper to tell them I'd pay the rest after I fished.

Just after I got under way, my bow light went out. I shut down the big motor, jiggled the light, and it came back on. I headed off again, and the light went off again. Another jiggle and I was finally on my way.

I got to my favorite spot, turned off the big motor, unhooked my kill switch, removed my life vest, and eased the trolling motor into the water. I picked up my favorite rod and reel and started to cast, but the last time I'd fished, someone had messed with the cast control knob, and the rod twisted from my grip right into the water.

To understand the next part, you have to know one thing. I look as though I'm trying to smuggle a twenty-pound rump roast out of the grocery store under my shirt. This was especially important that morning because the long arm of the law of gravity was about to catch up with me.

The rod was slowly slipping below the surface of the water not far from the boat, so I lay down over the edge of the gunwale and made a desperate reach for it. Got it! This is where gravity got me and helped me slip over the gunwale and into the lake. I got the rod. But somewhere in the water were two treble hooks, and I had to get my big behind back into the boat. I pushed the rod over onto the deck and worked my way around the front past the trolling motor and back to the big motor. There I found the cavitation plate with my foot, grabbed the top of the motor, and pulled.

After the third try, I was back in the boat with everything wet—jeans, shirt, tennis shoes, wallet, hat—where's my hat? Oh, well, at least my rod and I were back aboard. However, I was wet and the breeze was blowing over me. Now I needed to relieve myself, so I laid my rod down to take care of business. It was still dark and the boat had drifted who knows how far, when suddenly it found the bank. You guessed it. I was overboard again.

It did take care of one problem. I no longer needed to relieve myself. I moved to the front of the boat, picked up my rod, and trolled down to the next boathouse. I made a spectacular cast to the front of the dock and began my retrieve. The lure came to an abrupt halt right in front of the dock. I set the hook, but, damn, it was only a rope dangling beneath the dock. I trolled over to it, lay down on the deck, and reached under the water to unhook the lure. Why I was still holding the rope at this point is beyond me, but I did pick up the rod and set it out of the way. As I rolled over on the deck, I accidentally hit the trolling motor control button. The boat started to move and I realized I was still holding that rope. Back into the water I went.

For the next six hours, I was the most careful fisherman you would ever encounter. I stayed as far away from the edge of the boat as I possibly could. I did not cast toward

Overboard

anything. I did not catch many fish, but I did see a beautiful sunrise, listened to heaven sing through the throats of songbirds, and witnessed the birth of a new day, which I would spend with my loved ones.

As I prepared to head home to fulfill the terms of the bargain with my wife, I thought I ought to go back to my starting hole and give it another try. What the heck, right? Maybe things had settled down—they couldn't get worse, could they?—and Mister Big would be there, waiting for me. I shut down the big motor when I got there and crawled carefully to the front deck and held onto the pro pole as I eased the trolling motor into the water. Still holding on to that pole for dear life, I looked across the water and there, lo and behold, was my fishing cap floating serenely on the surface.

The next time someone tells you that a bad day of fishing is better than a good day working, tell my story. But I guess it wasn't such a bad day after all—I did get back my favorite hat.

Dry Clothing
It's a good idea to keep dry clothing in the boat, just in case you need it.

"Reeds like a *rod* bent double drew me to the spot."

IN THE "PATTERN" sport of bass fishing, there may be many places around a lake with similar conditions where at least a few fish are almost guaranteed. It may be every fallen tree in the water or only those on south shores. Small patches of red rock scattered throughout the fishery may be the key. It may not be the rock shore or the clay bank next to it but the transition between the two. It may be a single underwater rock pile with access to deep water or a long point that ends in an underwater river channel. All hot spots seem to have one thing in common: they are different from the surrounding area.

Do the Right Thing
Good technique spells success, and success inspires confidence.

Finding and fishing these spots well take common sense and recognition of what drew the fish there in the first place. There are times when no matter what we do, we "catch 'em good" at a hot spot. Even in those situations, more careful thought would probably increase the number, and maybe even the size, of the bass taken.

Approach the spot knowing fish are there. Work your bait as if a fish were looking at it every second it's in the water. Shut down the gas motor farther away than usual. Make long casts in your initial approach, and be quiet. Go as if you're sneaking into the house after a late night. Fish the outside edges first, working to the heart of the spot. Wear clothes that blend into the sky. Watch your shadow and, like a top gun pilot, come in low with the sun at your back. If possible (and if you have a good livewell), do not release fish until you leave. They may not talk to each other, but the caught fish you stressed may release substances into the water that cause the others to lose their appetite.

After thoroughly fishing the spot, come back later. You probably didn't catch all the resident fish, and those you traumatized by catching their buddy may have gotten over it. Additionally, the bass you did catch once lived somewhere else, and if conditions don't radically change, you can bet sooner or later new fish will move in.

If a spot that seemed to hold a large number of fish turns off, look around. Bass are very territorial and generally don't move far. You may find they just left the top of your rock pile for the deep cut thirty feet away.

Finally, savor it, enjoy it, and be sure to smile a lot. Hot-spot fishing is pretty cool.

Finding the Spot
A sun-warmed stump in a northern cove could be the right place to look for a spring hot spot.

FAST WORK
Hot-Spot Fishing

"I caught a glimpse of that big head in the shade, looking up at me."

Big Bass, Big Money

Hours before the first loon calls to its mate,

we're out of beds, pulling on our clothes, and spilling from motel rooms into the parking lot that is filling with other bass anglers preparing for battle. It's tournament morning!

Like any big-time athlete, the experienced bass angler thrives on the rush. The good-natured kibitzing over a cup of Java helps to reign in the competitive fever, and a low murmur of voices barely carries through the predawn fog. The silence is broken only now and again by the whisper of dew-blanketed tarps sliding off the boats and the muffled thud of something being dropped into a boat or truck bed. Once the first rigs begin to pull out of the lot and onto the boulevard, the pace quickens. With the final tasks, like loading rods and reels and soft tackle bags and, for some, a last trip into the room to brush their teeth, the relaxed, almost meditative pace of an hour ago has taken on a sudden sense of urgency.

Somewhere on that trip down the road in the early-morning gloom, a transformation begins in the cabs of those large rigs—a metamorphosis from fisherman to competitor. The adrenaline begins to course into every bass angler's system, tightening stomachs and leaving the fingertips icy cold. Like any big-time athlete, each experienced bass angler thrives on this rush.

At the launch site, handshakes and jokes renew many an old friendship in the fog along the lakeshore. Boaters meet up with their angling partners and quietly begin to finalize their strategy for the day. If you watch carefully, you'll see some of the younger competitors straining to catch glimpses of their heroes prepping tackle and boats. Mentors move among the groups in the darkness, seeking out their inexperienced charges with last-minute instructions and words of encouragement.

Like a grand parade, the long line of expensive rigs snakes through the parking lot, each waiting its turn to use the limited number of launch ramps. This carefully orchestrated army, tow vehicles and their accompanying trailers, moves with purpose and great haste. While on the lake early launches wait, exhaust from their outboards hovers in the air like a ghostly fog and reflections of their colored navigation lights swirl on the water's surface, looking hauntingly like van Gogh's *Starry Night*. On board, anglers carefully choose lures, re-tie knots, and meticulously set rods and reels in their proper places. Awaiting the bullhorn blast—the call to attention—younger competitors work hard to calm their nerves and look cool, while veterans confidently sip coffee from "no spill" cups.

Eventually the call to attention blasts. At the tournament director's word, all outboards go silent. Under the cobalt blue predawn sky anglers synchronize watches, offer up a prayer, and then a worn-out recording of the national anthem crackles out over the water. Finally, called by launch order, each boat idles by tournament organizers for one last inspection. Passing anglers open all livewells and display lanyards in response to the event director's orders: "Kill switches and livewells, gentlemen."

PRO TIPS

In fall, when water temperatures drop, riprap and rock are good areas to start looking for active bass.

ANXIOUS WAITING

The most nervous time in a tournament is just before "send-off." It's the only time a competitor can look around and see just how much he is up against.

"He *danced* on his tail and threw off *diamonds* of sunlight."

The mandatory pass-by completed, anglers check zippers and snaps, pull drawstrings tight, and ready themselves for launch. The long line of bass boats, marked only by tall rear navigational lights, promenades out to the marker buoys that remind boaters of the strict no-wake zone at the mouth of the cove. Glancing over at their comrades, drivers bellow one last warning: "Ready?" Many simply nod their heads, while others shout, "Let's do it!"

Immediately after completely clearing the buoys, the 150-horsepower outboards roar to life. The huge sleds rise out of the water, climb on pad, and race the sun to the first "honey hole."

An equal number of boats charge up and down the lake like a pack of stock cars, three sleds racing side by side into the waking morn. A single sled peels off and comes to rest at the front of a small cove. Another veers right and disappears up a long tributary arm. Another two miles of lakeshore passes before the last craft falls off pad and slides to a stop. The driver unzips his life jacket and jumps up on the bow. Before a single word is passed, the trolling motor is dropped into the slick water and both anglers have their rods in hand. The race is on.

Dew-draped twigs of flooded brush and the thin veil of fog give the shallow flat a dreamlike look. An unexpected splash, just beyond the anglers' dismal field of vision, hints at early activity. Down the bank, a blue heron barks out a protest and takes to flight.

The rich odor of shad fills the air. With a quick roll of his wrist, the lead angler sends his bait toward the bank. Sounding much like a soup can pushed down an alley by a summer breeze, a buzzbait struggles to stay on top of the water surface. Using his rod tip, the bass angler directs the noisy lure's path so it brushes against the flooded timber.

Suddenly, the water surrounding the lure boils and the buzzbait disappears. The rod bows to the unseen power beneath the dark water. Instinctively, the bass fights to reach the safety of nearby timber. The angler knows he must quickly turn the predator's head up toward the surface, clear of the heavy cover. The fast tip of the rod lunges forward and snaps back with every movement of the fish. Suddenly, the big bass changes strategy. Like a missile, the female rockets toward the surface and breaches. With violent headshakes and gill plates flared, she is trying desperately to throw the hook that is lodged in the roof of her mouth. Each jump, shake, and tail thrust is acknowledged with shouts of approval.

Eventually, the fatigued bass is brought to the side of the boat. On both knees and stooped over, the angler takes a deep breath and reaches into the water, his thumb and fingers locked firmly around the bass's lower jaw. Carefully, gently, he lifts the exhausted fish to the livewell and looks up at his grinning partner. "It's going to be a real good day!"

After a deep breath, he picks up his rod and reel and, with shaking hands, attempts to duplicate his

success. Unfortunately, as often happens, the promising water fails to meet the anglers' expectations. A single, undersized bass and a halfhearted swipe at a passing spinnerbait are all the two anglers could pull from the flat. Time to move to another hole.

The sun has reduced the fog to a thin shroud. The lead angler hooks his bait onto the lure keep, makes a number of quick wraps with the line around the rod, and secures the rod on the flipping deck. The second angler follows the first angler's lead. "Whatcha got in mind?" he queries.

"I have a few more flats just like this that have consistently held bass in practice," the first answers. "If they fail us, we go to your spots."

With a low rumble, the big outboard responds to the turn of the key. The throttle is pushed forward, and the nose of the fiberglass sled rises skyward before sliding back down. Although neither angler will submit to the creeping self-doubt, both begin mentally reviewing what they know, theorizing about what is happening and calculating what adjustments might be necessary. This process of mental computation is a big part of tournament fishing and can be either the angler's salvation or undoing.

Eventually, the big rig slows and comes off plane near another timbered flat back of a tributary creek. This place looks promising. The sun has now almost completely burned away the fog. Exchanging a buzzbait for a shallow running crankbait, the lead prepares to cast. His partner chooses to continue with the spinnerbait. Together, the two competitors probe the cover-rich water for its hidden treasure—black bass.

Finally, a second keeper-size bass strikes the spinnerbait and manages to hook itself. The smallish fish is rushed to the boat and quickly swung onboard. "It's not much," confirms the grateful angler, "but it's a keeper."

Dozens of fruitless casts, lure changes, and color, blade, and size combinations all answer hope with futility. The anglers

WEIGHING THE WINNERS

The weigh-in at the end of a sun-filled tournament day is the culmination of an experience where everybody is a winner (facing page). By the time the last bass is weighed, most competitors are already thinking about the next day on the water.

exchange their lures for slower, more deliberate presentations and again test the more promising spots on the flat, but to no avail. The bright, cloudless sky expanding above them is an indication of the rising barometer. Sensing the changes in their watery environment, the bass have become more cautious.

With just three hours remaining in the event, the competitors know their next decision may be critical. They decide to try deeper, open water, knowing that the deeper fish are normally less affected by changing conditions.

They point the boat to a stock tank dam rising to within twenty feet of the surface and just a mile down the lake. As they slowly approach, the driver watches his electronic graph and begins marking the structure with buoys. "There it is," he says quietly. "Let's get to work."

With renewed optimism, the two competitors grab their rods and take up their position on the two flipping decks. Almost immediately, the first hookup is made. A nice sixteen-inch bass is muscled to the boat and hastily placed in a waiting livewell. Five more casts result in an additional three undersized bass.

Eventually, the bite slows and the two anglers struggle to place the final two legal-size fish in the boat. The senior angler warns, "We've got time for another cast or two and then we have to go."

The two casts turn into a half-dozen more, and the anglers are forced to rush back to the scales. At the weigh-in site, the catch of fellow anglers confirms their story of a tough bite day. While the five-pounder wasn't good enough to win the big bass award, it was indeed big enough to put the two men in the money. Checks in hand, they proclaim, "Next time, guys. Next time!" It's that hope or expectation, rooted in past failures and successes, that fuels the obsession of tournament fishing. ◢ —*Paul Cañada*

"I set the *hook*
and that largemouth
jerked back with
angry *resolve*."

LONG-TIME BASS pro Roland Martin was practicing for a tournament on the Mississippi. His son, Scott, was also competing, and they had heard that Lake Millwood, located 120 miles south by water, held good fish. Since the Mississippi was very low, Roland and his partner trailered his boat south and launched near the lake. Scott decided to run the river and experience the trip before the tournament.

The last day of practice, they met on the lake and traded information. Scott had found a bank going out of Millwood that held solid fish. He also told Roland they didn't need to fish that bank that day. In fact, he asked that they stay off of it. Roland agreed.

Scott left, and Roland continued to scratch fish. He mused aloud that Scott might not have caught a fish. He might just have felt a bite and never set the hook. "Maybe," he said, "we should check to be sure they were bass." His partner reminded him that Scott had specified the size of the bass, so he must have taken at least one. Roland said,

"Well, maybe that was the only fish, and if we don't check, Scott might waste a lot of time." His partner voted no.

Roland got quiet, thinking. Then he said, "We might have fished the area anyway, just by chance." Again his partner voted no. The odds they would have stumbled upon that bank, miles from where they sat, were minuscule. "But," his partner said, "you're the fancy-pants bass pro, so you decide and I'll keep my mouth shut." That was it—they were off to the spot.

They hadn't thrown three casts when Roland hooked a three-pound bass. He fought the fish to the boat, where his swivel pin snap opened and the fish got away with his crankbait. They left the bank and later found a strong pattern on two underwater rock piles.

The next day, Roland caught a good limit off those rocks. After the weigh-in, Scott walked up hotter than a nine-pound bass in two feet of water. "We're going to dance sideways here, Dad." He was almost shouting. Roland gave Scott his full attention.

It seems Scott fished that bank and came across a three-pound bass half-dead on the surface, with a crankbait hanging out of its mouth. He said he released the fish, but at first was puzzled, since there was no line attached to the bait. Then he remembered Roland's swivel-pin practicing style. He looked at him and said, "Darn it, Dad. After I asked you not to, you went and fished that bank, didn't you?"

Roland seemed to shrink and became awfully interested in his feet. After an awkward silence, he looked up and said, "Son, did you bring me my crankbait?"

Moment of Decision
The appeal of bass fishing is in its uncertainty. Some days you can get everything right, and they still decide not to bite.

THE IRRESISTIBLE LURE
Temptation

Aft port
storage
locker

Dual pump

Ice chest

Bucket seat

Folding swim step

Fishing seat

225 hp
outboard
motor

Battery storage
compartment

Aft starboard storage locker

Bass Boat

DREAM BOAT

Modern bass boats are literally fishing platforms.
The boats' highly sophisticated systems maximize
the skills of the angler to approach, find, and
capture bass. These boats allow the anglers
to reach fish, safely and dependably far
from the morning launch, with a top
speed of more than seventy miles per
hour and a cruising range easily in excess of
two hundred miles without refueling.

Truck and trailer
A dependable vehicle gets the angler to the water and,
even more importantly, allows easy launching and retrieving
of the three-thousand-pound boat.

Lighted glove box with power outlet

Interior deck lights

Below deck water-tight storage areas

Port rod storage locker

Casting platform

Removable seat

Troll motor

Duplicate electronic control panel

Liquid crystal sonar unit

"Black" light for night fishing.

Starboard locker

Dash command center

Sonar/GPS unit

Trolling Motor
The electric troll motor can be operated by a foot pedal. It allows an angler to quietly and effortlessly fish large stretches of water, typically shorelines, while prospecting for bass.

IN THE EARLY YEARS of bass tournaments, many events were blemished by cheating and scandals. Some competitors caught fish prior to a tournament, placed them on stringers, and then returned to collect them during competition. Today, tournament organizers carefully administer the events to eliminate all opportunities for cheating. Most national tournament trails are as professionally administered as other professional sport competitions.

Rules about equipment and how fish are caught ensure fair and safe competition, and cheating is easily exposed. Off-limit

Personal Best
Sometimes a young angler has no better use for an old shoestring than to use it to measure each catch against his personal best, marked by a knot.

periods restrict anglers' on-water practice time just prior to competition, and in many events, anglers are prohibited from soliciting assistance or advice from locals and guides.

In most competitions, anglers are limited to artificial baits manipulated by rod and reel only. Many events prohibit the use of nets and any assistance from partners or observers when landing hooked bass.

The rules are written to protect both competitors and their catch. At almost every level of competition, bass anglers are required to wear U.S. Coast Guard–approved personal flotation devices and have the lanyard

connected to the emergency stop, or "kill switch," when the large outboard is under power. Rules require that tournament catches remain alive and well so they can be safely released later. All contestants must have properly operating, aerated livewells. Some states require that all bass caught in a tournament be released and that fish caught during the summer months not be held by contestants more than six hours. Some club-level tournaments require competitors to measure fish just after they're caught, release the fish immediately, and use the length to calculate the weight. Significant penalties, such as loss of fish

and/or weight, are assessed to anglers who weigh in dead fish, have too many fish in the livewell, or attempt to weigh in undersized fish.

Understandably, scoring varies among professional tournament circuits, bass clubs, and special "big bass" events. Normally, rules and scoring reflect the emphasis of the organization. In "big bass" events, an angler's finish is based on the weight of the largest single bass caught during competition.

In tournament trail and club events, the total weight of the best fish, as determined by the bag and length limit, determines the winner. Additionally, competitors are awarded points based on their finish in each event, and the points are tallied throughout the season. The competitor with the most points at the end of the season wins the Angler of the Year award, and a predetermined number of top finishers compete in the year-end championship.

Professional Expertise
Women make up an increasing number of contestants at bass tournaments, and it is a sport in which anyone can contend for a championship.

BASS TOURNAMENTS
Rules of the Game

AS THE BOW of the twenty-foot bass boat lifts off the water, the driver and his angling partner zip up their jackets and tighten the drawstrings of their hoods in preparation for the long, cold trip back to the weigh-in site.

Tucked away in the comfort and security of a large livewell, five sizable bass—the fruits of the day's efforts—are at rest. The livewell allows bass anglers to keep their catch alive while they continue fishing through the day.

With the adoption of catch and release, a livewell became vital equipment on a modern bass boat. But proper care for a catch begins well before the fish is brought on board. Anglers know that every time they place a dry hand on a bass, drop a fish on the boat carpet, or slap one against a measuring stick, they damage the bass's valuable slime coat. The slime coat is an excreted mucus with antibacterial properties that inhibit the growth of fungus and bacteria. Infections often set in where slime has been unintentionally removed by careless handling.

Experienced fishermen reduce the damage to the slime coat by wetting their hands and measuring devices before handling fish. More important, anglers ensure the slime coat of captive bass remains healthy by using a chemical formula for livewells that stimulates the continued excretion of the mucus.

Because bass are wild creatures, they require special handling and care when held captive. Although livewell deaths are usually the result of poor handling and care, bass often die days after being released as a result of captivity-related stress. Chemical treatments greatly increase the odds of survival by enhancing the livewell environment and reducing many causes of shock. Some treatments have a tranquilizer that slows the bass's metabolism and replaces critical electrolytes lost during the fight. Both help prevent shock when the fish is introduced to the livewell environment.

A major killer of tournament bass is the hot, stagnant water found in many livewells. As the temperature of livewell water climbs, its oxygen-carrying capacity begins to diminish. High water temperatures and low levels of dissolved oxygen are fatal to those fish already suffering from physiological stress.

It's important to monitor the livewell environment when lake surface water reaches above the mid-seventies. By installing an inexpensive digital livewell thermometer and adding ice at timely intervals, anglers can keep water temperatures down. Automatic aeration and circulation systems and chemical treatments also help improve dissolved oxygen levels. In the end, the best-equipped livewells are only as good as the angler who is monitoring and maintaining them.

Bass Livewell
Dependable aeration in the well keeps the fish happy, with high oxygen content and survival rates.

BRINGING THEM BACK

Live in the Well

wet hands and mindful of exposed hooks, most people can carefully secure a thumbhold on the lower jaw of the bass. The next step is to gently but quickly remove the hook with pliers or a hemostat. Once the hook is out, it is vital to revive the fish before releasing it. If necessary this can be done by gently holding the bass at the base of the tail and covering the nose and eyes to allow the fish to calm down. This only takes a minute or so. When fully revived, it will gladly swim away from a gentle hold.

Tender Loving Care
Fish should be handled as little as possible. If a bass shows signs of shock, (facing page), sometimes a gentle back-and-forth movement in the water can revive it.

HAVING REGAINED its strength, the large female bolts from human grasp and disappears into the deeper water. The smiling bass angler dries his hands with a towel and says, "Until next time!" That simple act of catch and release gives modern fishermen more satisfaction than they would ever get from the traditional stringer photo of days past. The practice of setting free a potential wallhanger or sizable meal is an act of good stewardship that protects the future of the sport by preserving the larger, more prolific spawners.

But safely releasing a large fish requires some special care. Bass suffer physiological stress during the fight following the hookup and during handling. It's important to take care of the fish once it is caught. With

GOOD STEWARDSHIP
Catch & Release

AFTERWORD
Memories that Endure

On a Valentine's Day Saturday more than a decade ago, I was competing in a typical club tournament in Southern California. These monthly contests form a bass club's *raison d'être*. Competitors often set their lives, and that of anyone they can influence, around the club tournament schedule. Weddings are planned, vacations are taken, and even career changes are formulated around these events.

Chris, my wife of less than a year, was my nonfishing partner that day. Bass had been in a prespawn mode for weeks. Small males prospected for bedding areas in very shallow water whereas the untouchable females were suspended much deeper, religiously keeping to their annual hunger strike. The females were poised in the starting blocks, waiting for that minute change of temperature and light to convince them it was time to get in the game. They would sense when it was right in every cove and shoreline.

The instant the commitment was made, the need to reproduce the species would touch off a dramatic increase in activity, but the signal hadn't come yet.

Huge cumulus clouds floated like gigantic galleons above us. Rain had come and gone and was possible again. Competitors concentrated on the small males, rightly assuming the females were uncatchable. Most figured a ten-pound total on the five-fish limit would put them in the front of the pack at the end. Working hard, with very light line, I had three fish in my livewell by 9:30 A.M. Each was two pounds or so, and I was on track for a decent finish.

I must have been a little unbalanced by Chris's presence in the boat, because at midmorning I did the unthinkable. I stopped fishing, put down my rod, and handed her a surprise Valentine's Day gift from my rod locker. When she removed the wrapping, she discovered the box for a first-rate Shimano fishing reel. Gamely trying to hide her obvious disappointment, and probably a vivid thought that this marriage might not have been such a swell idea, she opened the package to discover a small but over-the-budget diamond ring. She still wears it today.

It seemed that at the instant of her discovery the sun broke from behind the clouds to light her smile. I looked at the face I loved and had an inspiration; the waiting female bass might have been jump-started by this change of light and the brighter texture of daylight into the shallows.

I hurriedly put down my finesse rod and looked around for standing tules in the shallow water nearby. Chris put the ring on her finger and held it out for me to see. I said, "Honey pie, maybe those females have been coaxed into the bedding area."

"What?" She was obviously confused.

"I could take about an hour from this small fish stuff, look for bigger females shallow; and if I'm wrong, I can still recover from the lost time."

PRO TIPS

Be patient. Don't hurry your retrieve, and fish an area throroughly if you've had a bite there. Return to the area later in the day and try again.

TEAMWORK

When families enjoy the sport together, no matter who goes home with bragging rights, everyone shares the happy memories.

She was looking down, turning the ring in the sunlight, but her face cleared. "Great idea," she said. I think I could have said I was running away to Arkansas and her reply would have been the same. She was probably really talking about the ring.

A watery explosion met my third pitch with a fat, ugly, plastic worm on 20-pound test line into the shallow-water cover. I thought I had spooked a carp until my line moved sharply and a quick hookset soon put a four-pound bass in the boat. I had not seen a bass weighing over two pounds in weeks. The females were shallow, and they had an attitude!

Later, I deliberately walked to the scales last. A good friend was in the lead with five nice males that weighed just over eleven pounds. When I asked for two live-catch bags to transfer my fish from boat to scale, more than a few people looked up. The leader seemed to lose a little color. Heart pounding, but looking as casual as a major league ballplayer after a nice catch, I handed both bags to the tournament director.

I had fed no hungry children that day. I had rescued no fair maiden from the path of a speeding train. The world—and my life—had stayed pretty much the same, really. But on this one unforgettable day, on this particular lake, I had thought my way to a tournament victory; and better yet, I had done it myself.

I can still clearly picture that short pitch of my bait alongside the tule that day. The explosion of water was so unexpected, my hookset and reaction so automatic, that I didn't appreciate what happened until that female was thrashing in the boat. My adrenaline kicked in about then, but I didn't notice how much my hands were shaking until my next short cast hit the water.

Today when I see that ring on my wife's finger, I'm sure my thoughts are quite different from hers, but it was part of one of those precious life experiences for both of us that the pursuit of bass seems to generate like no other. ❨ —*Kevin Mineo*

THE PUBLISHERS WOULD like to thank the following people for their help and advice: Debra Dean of *Honey Hole Magazine*; Clyde Harbin; Jamie Chatham; Allen Forshage; Scott Rob of Legend Creek Outfitters; Pete Press; and Roger Rucci of Joe's Sporting Goods.

SPECIAL THANKS goes to Bill Lindner and Mike Hehner of Bill Lindner Photography for their special request photography, advice, and research, and for always being available on this project; to Ron Fingers at Redpine, Inc. for his extra efforts to get illustrations done on time; and to Kevin Mineo for his many hours of extra research and for generously providing his boat for photography.

"Overboard" is reprinted with permission from *Honey Hole Magazine* (http://www.honeyholemagazine.com).

Acknowledgments

PHOTOGRAPHERS

Mike Acklin
14

Jack Bissell Photography
62b, 63

Paul A. Cañada
140–141, 172–173, 175

Willard Clay
72–73, 82–83, 114–115

©Creative Publishing
International/Bill Lindner
Photography
14–15, 23b, 34b, 35, 68a,
75a, 113, 184

©Dorling Kindersley
38–39c, 32–33b, 26–27a

Tom Evans Photography
1, 17b, 36–37, 50a, 53a,
54a, 55, 58a, 58b, 84b,
90–91, 91a, 92a, 99,

120–121, 120, 124a, 128b,
130b, 139a, 143b, 146–147,
152b, 152a, 160–161, 165,
168a, 178a, 179, 180b,
180a, 184–185

David Friend
84a, 112, 138, 170–171a,
170–171b, 171

Ethan Gordon
18b

Charles Gurche
79a

Doug Hannon
19, 118–119

©Bill Lindner Photography
10–11, 12–13, 13, 16–17,
17a, 18a, 20–21, 24–25,
30–31, 40a, 40b, 41a, 44b,
44c, 44d, 44a, 45, 46–47,
48, 50b, 51, 53b, 54b, 59,
60–61, 62a, 62c, 64–65,
68b, 69b, 70b, 70c, 70a,

74a, 74b, 76–77, 78b,
80–81, 88–89, 91b, 94a,
94a, 96a, 96b, 97, 98,
98–99, 102a, 102b,
102–103, 103, 108b, 108a,
109b, 109a, 110–111, 123b,
128a, 129, 130a, 131, 132,
133, 134–135, 136a, 137,
139b, 142, 144, 145, 148,
149, 156–157, 156, 158,
159, 162a, 162b, 163,
164–165, 168, 169, 174a,
174b, 176–177, 178b, 181,
187, 191

Larry Mishkar/Innerspace
Visions
28b, 42–43

Lynn and Donna
Rogers/northart.com
6–7, 52–53, 153, 92b

Dale C. Spartas, DCS Photo Inc.,
Spartasphoto@imt.net
48–49, 56–57, 66, 69a, 71,
88, 96c, 124b, 154–155

Richard Hamilton Smith
2–3, 4–5, 79b, 85, 93,
104–105, 123a, 126–127,
136b, 150–151, 182–183

Doug Stamm
23a, 28a, 34a, 78a, 86–87,
95, 100–101, 106a, 106b,
122–123, 125, 166–167,
186, 192

ILLUSTRATORS

Ron Finger/Redpine, Inc.
26–27b, 32–33a, 37–38a,
41b, 75b, 78c, 106–107,
107, 112b, 136c

Larry Tople
8–9, 22, 29, 67, 116–117,
143a

Note: *Letters refer to the position of the photo on the page, beginning from left to right and proceeding from top to bottom.*

Photo Credits

Index